HOW TOYOTA BECAME #1

DAVID MAGEE

HOW

||||||||||||||||||||||||||||||||||||||||||||||||||||||||||||||||||||||

TOYOTA

||||||||||||||||||||||||||||||||||||||||||||||||||||||||||||||||||||||

BECAME #1

LEADERSHIP LESSONS

FROM THE WORLD'S

GREATEST CAR

COMPANY

PORTFOLIO

PORTFOLIO
Published by the Penguin Group
Penguin Group (USA) Inc., 375 Hudson Street,
New York, New York 10014, U.S.A.
Penguin Group (Canada), 90 Eglinton Avenue East, Suite 700,
Toronto, Ontario, Canada M4P 2Y3
(a division of Pearson Penguin Canada Inc.)
Penguin Books Ltd, 80 Strand, London WC2R 0RL, England
Penguin Ireland, 25 St. Stephen's Green, Dublin 2, Ireland
(a division of Penguin Books Ltd)
Penguin Books Australia Ltd, 250 Camberwell Road, Camberwell,
Victoria 3124, Australia
(a division of Pearson Australia Group Pty Ltd)
Penguin Books India Pvt Ltd, 11 Community Centre, Panchsheel Park,
New Delhi–110 017, India
Penguin Group (NZ), 67 Apollo Drive, Rosedale, North Shore 0632,
Auckland, New Zealand (a division of Pearson New Zealand Ltd.)
Penguin Books (South Africa) (Pty) Ltd, 24 Sturdee Avenue,
Rosebank, Johannesburg 2196, South Africa

Penguin Books Ltd, Registered Offices:
80 Strand, London WC2R 0RL, England

First published in 2007 by Portfolio,
a member of Penguin Group (USA) Inc.

1 3 5 7 9 10 8 6 4 2

LIBRARY OF CONGRESS CATALOGING IN PUBLICATION DATA
Magee, David, date.
How Toyota became #1 : leadership lessons from the world's greatest car company / David Magee.
p. cm.
Includes bibliographical references and index.
ISBN 978-1-59184-179-1
1. Toyota Jidosha Kabushiki Kaisha—Management. 2. Automobile industry and trade—Japan—Management—
Case studies. 3. Automobile industry and trade—United States—Management—Case studies. 4. Leadership—
Case studies. 5. Customer service—Case studies. I. Title. II. Title: How Toyota became number one.
HD9710.J34T6528 2007
658.4'092—dc22   2007018556

Printed in the United States of America
Set in ITC New Baskerville

For KRM

Everyone should tackle some great project at least once in their life.

—Sakichi Toyoda,
father of Kiichiro Toyoda,
the founder of Toyota

CONTENTS

|||||||||||||||||||||||||||||||||||||||

HOW TOYOTA BECAME #1

INTRODUCTION

|||||||||||||||||||||||||||||||||||||||||||||||||

This is not the book I set out to write. The original idea was simply to compare Toyota to industry competitors like General Motors, Ford, and Nissan, showing how the company bested its peers year after year in a multitude of categories. It was going to be another manufacturing how-to guide for industry types.

While not exciting, such an approach made sense, since, by 2007, few companies in the world were more talked about in business and media circles than Toyota. The company made headlines earlier that year when it announced an annual production and sales objective which, if met, would make the company the largest carmaker in the world.

Attempting a double-jump leapfrog past longtime global giants Ford (the world's perennial number two) and General Motors (the world's perennial number one), Toyota's rise to the top turned heads from Detroit to Denver to Dubai. Consider this: Ford, which once held sway over 25 percent of all car and truck sales, had tenaciously held on to second place behind GM for more than 70 years.

But as Toyota surged, Ford struggled like never before, closing plants and eliminating thousands of white- and blue-collar jobs. New Chief Executive Officer Alan Mulally even suggested the company would not be profitable again until at least 2009. GM was not faring much better. Company chairman and CEO Rick Wagoner stated publicly that maintaining the number one spot as the world's largest carmaker was of paramount importance, but grudgingly admitted that doing so would be difficult (Ford wasn't the only company closing plants and laying off thousands of workers).

Toyota was heading to the top—a rather significant accomplishment for a company that for decades had been perceived as formidable but small, something of a niche conglomerate, for lack of a better phrase.

Sales dominance, however, was only part of the story. Toyota proved to industry insiders some time ago that it had the power to rewrite the rules of the industry. For example, followers of the auto industry had long believed that, because of its economically sensitive nature, it was a cyclical business. That's the way it had been for as long as anyone could remember. Influences such as oil and steel prices, consumer confidence, interest rates and the like had the capacity to dictate buying patterns which would affect sales, profits, and so on.

A fifteen-year sales chart for Toyota, however, reveals a very different picture. Despite what was happening in the economy, Toyota's annual net earnings appeared to be quite consistent: a steady elevation over most of that period, with a dramatic jump northward toward the end. Nothing about Toyota's results were cyclical. Their sales were eclipsed when GM and Ford reported their best years, but they never suffered the deep setbacks during the tough years that sent shock waves through the senior management teams of GM and Ford. In fact, during those "tough" years there was barely a blip in Toyota's sales at all.

Dig deeper into Toyota's history and one finds steady growth, much-better-than-industry-average shareholder returns, off-the-charts consumer loyalty ratings, and some of the happiest employees in the world. It's no wonder, then, that the company has captured the attention of some of Harvard's top business school professors as well as some of the best-selling business authors in the world (such as *Good to Great* author Jim Collins).

However, even I was surprised at what I found as I interviewed key managers at Toyota. Despite the company's incredibly successful, even meteoric rise, it was nearly impossible to get anyone inside the company to talk about the numbers.

The reason, I learned, was that the criteria and qualities leading to Toyota's rise to the top had little to do with sales results or profit margins. Numbers are simply by-products of daily work, and not the key to competitive greatness.

The story lines of most importance in revealing the real nature of an organization lie far beneath the numbers. Again, data are important, but they serve more as validation than substance. Once I uncovered this essential truth, my approach to this book took a decidedly different turn.

Even considering the iconic, beloved, and time-tested John Deere brand, or the Japanese automaker Nissan under bold leadership, never before have I studied a company with more valuable management lessons to offer than Toyota. More than an automaker or manufacturing company, Toyota, as the following pages will reveal, is a professional lifestyle—a proven and time-tested way of progression, improvement, ambition, and betterment.

I have read many business books—dozens, in fact—and have even dished out a few myself, but I must admit that I had never before run across the single company or person that offered much more than a few handy nuggets worth keeping.

I found amusement, for instance, learning about Southwest Airlines' mushy style, but those lessons can only get someone so far. Similarly, I found it entertaining to learn why people are willing to pay more for tractors painted green than those painted with other colors, yet the lessons did not inspire me to do better work or pursue a more rewarding path. Such was not the case after I embarked on the path that took me to research and write this book.

Not the Biggest, Just the Best

While sitting in Toyota's New York office one morning and casually talking with Jim Press, president of Toyota Motor North America and a senior managing director of Toyota Motor Corporation* (the first non-Japanese to hold such a distinction), I had an epiphany of sorts. Listening to Mr. Press speak about Toyota's way of doing business—"We don't want to be the biggest, just the best" and "Why should you watch the stock price? It leads to bad decisions"—I realized the company's business mantra is not so much about quarterly earnings and net profit as it is about striving each day to develop people. It is not so much a business plan as a philosophy. There is greater commitment exhibited in internal company statements regarding the environment than in any letter to shareholders, yet Toyota's stock price keeps going up.

It was at that moment that I abandoned my original plan of writing another industry-specific guide that would be of great interest to a relatively small number of people. Instead, I sought to shine the light on the most valuable and useful leadership lessons to be learned from Toyota's unique approach to business. I knew if I was successful the result would be a book that would be of interest to a great number of people who, like me, are hungry for more direction, a sharper competitive edge, and a clearer road map to personal success and fulfillment.

This book is the result. Not corporate hagiography, since, as you will quickly learn, the company is far from perfect; and not a corporate biography that weaves together every move and milestone of a company founded between the first and second world wars. Instead, what follows are the principles, lessons, and strategies that helped make one company one of the most successful and inspirational in the world—and without a doubt the number one car company on the planet.

*After this book was written, Jim Press left his position with Toyota to become vice-president and co-chairman of Chrysler. All interviews were conducted while Press was still employed by Toyota.

1

||||||||||||||

Diligently Apply to the Right Pursuits

If we only tried to achieve the results and the objectives, then results and objectives would not be sustainable.

—Mitsuo Kinoshita, Toyota executive vice president

TOYOTA MAY BE the world's leading automobile manufacturer, but the company is about far more than cars. Some might assume that part of Toyota's success comes from its rich Japanese heritage and discipline, but few success stories can be explained away that easily. Besides, profitably designing, producing, and selling almost ten million cars each year while delighting the majority of its customers can never be considered easy.

Some might attribute the company's success to Toyota's efficient and unique manufacturing system, which continues to turn out some of the industry's most impressive cars. However, that's only a very small part of the company's strength. Managers who hope to emulate Toyota's success must look beyond its patented manufacturing system. The many pieces that comprise Toyota, from applications to management philosophies to products, combine to create a growth machine that is remarkably consistent. While its American counterparts are facing possible extinction, Toyota has not had a money-losing quarter in more than half a century. That's a remarkable achievement given the volatility and intensely competitive nature of the global automobile market.

How the company handles its new hires is just as important to its overall success as how the company manages parts flow at assembly plants. Similarly, the company's approach to partnerships and alliances is as important as its approach to quality. The secret to Toyota's success doesn't lie in any one of these areas but in how it approaches its business as a whole, with an underlying focus on "respect for people." That makes the lessons learned from Toyota's model as applicable to a bank or a retailer as to a manufacturer. By maintaining a focus on one very lofty ideal, and by implementing and maintaining a business structure that encourages every employee to be actively engaged in pursuing the company's goals, Toyota is developing into a self-regenerating internally combustive enterprise.

With its unique approach, Toyota has become one of the most admired, growing, and profitable corporations in the world, overcoming competitors and assuming a position of potentially unlimited global contribution in the twenty-first century. You'd be hard-pressed to get anyone working for the company to say so, however. Since Toyota's founding in the one-time countryside of Japan, and continuing throughout its worldwide operations today, the company has ignored the widely accepted definition of success. Instead, it collectively obsesses over something beyond profit margins and market share. To fully understand what Toyota is all about and how the different pieces of its corporate system work together in their shared pursuit, one must look back to the company's earliest days.

Pursue Perfection Relentlessly

Toyota started out as a family company. The founding family's leadership is still influencing the company's direction today, continuing a legacy that dates back to late nineteenth-century Japan. As a young man, Sakichi Toyoda (1867–1930), the son of a working-class carpenter, lived with his family several hours outside Tokyo in a small community that survived largely on the textile trade. Toyoda (the company name would later change) watched his mother and other women in the community struggle daily with the physically taxing hand-operated wooden looms, which required two hands to throw thread bobbins quickly back and forth from left to right. Motion was wasted in the process, making the jobs much more difficult than necessary.

Recognizing that the rudimentary machinery was damaging the physical well-being of his mother and the other women, Sakichi Toyoda began to search for ways to make their weaving jobs easier. A natural, self-taught inventor, he developed an improved loom that required only the simple motion of one hand, making the chore of loom operation much easier. But he was not satisfied with just one generation of loom improvement. He spent his days observing the women and put in long hours at night working to solve the problems he observed by developing better and continually improved machinery. Ultimately acquiring more than 100 patents and becoming etched in world history alongside names like Thomas Edison and

Henry Ford as influential men of creative commerce, Toyoda received his first loom patent in 1890—about the same time a man named Ransom Olds was building a steam-engine automobile in the United States.

Recognizing that his hand-operated looms could be further improved through mechanization—already adopted in the superior looms used in Europe and the United States—Sakichi Toyoda built Japan's first automatic loom after years of experimentation and development. He received a patent for the Toyoda Power Loom in 1896. Within a year the machinery was the centerpiece of Japan's burgeoning textile industry and his company, Toyoda Loom Works (later called Toyoda Automatic Loom Works), was among the most prosperous in the rural region.

Although his patented looms were a dramatic improvement for the weaving industry in Japan, they didn't hold up to the higher standards of looms in Europe and the United States. The complex contraptions often interrupted the work flow in the mills; broken threads held up the entire weaving process, and transferring spools caused excessive downtime. Parts were not interchangeable, and the design was not uniform. Sakichi Toyoda was not satisfied, believing he could do better and that the workers deserved better.

He traveled to Europe, studying looms made by Platt Brothers & Co. Ltd., the leading manufacturer in the United Kingdom. There, Toyoda gained exposure to Western business principles and philosophies, hungrily inquiring and continually absorbing new knowledge. The industrial age was well under way in the West, and both research and analysis of business practices and behaviors were readily available, something Toyoda had not yet found in Japan. He was particularly captivated by a noted nineteenth-century motivational management guru and author, Samuel Smiles (1812–1904).

A native of Scotland who studied medicine at the University of Edinburgh, Smiles wrote the first significant book in what would later become the extensive genre of motivational and personal improvement literature known as self-help. Still in print and widely read today, Smiles's aptly-titled book *Self-Help*, first published in 1859, was an immediate best seller in the United Kingdom.

"The spirit of self-help," Samuel Smiles once said, "is the root of all genuine growth in the individual; and, exhibited in the lives of many, it constitutes the true source of national vigour and strength."

Toyoda purchased an English copy of the book and is said by historians to have been heavily influenced by the work: It is the single bound manuscript on display at his birthplace in central Japan.

Sakichi Toyoda already had made a mark in his country. He was earning so much money that he could have easily accepted the state of his inventions and left his employees to work with the troublesome looms as best as they could. Instead, he continued to innovate. His looms continued to dramatically improve efficiency for the commercial weaving industry, becoming more advanced and earning him more money and recognition. His primary tenet for each succeeding generation of the loom was to reduce material waste and unnecessary human movement with better mechanization.

Even outside Japan, Toyoda was considered one of the world's most notable inventors and emerging industrialists, largely because he was not only a machinist but also an engaged student of business, constantly studying how people could make things more easily and efficiently. His studies eventually led him to adopt the principle of *jidoka*, or the ability of people to influence the quality of machine production at the source, one of the most important cornerstones of how Toyota manufactures products today.

But Sakichi Toyoda was also driven to improve the capability and quality of his tools. To do so, he sought the advice of the American engineer Charles A. Francis, who was teaching in Japan at the time. Not only did Toyoda allow Francis to retool Toyoda Loom Works' equipment, he peppered him with questions in an attempt to learn more about every step Francis took along the way. He paid careful attention to the American's manufacturing methods, which included reorganizing the line and redesigning the equipment so parts were both uniform and interchangeable. Within a few years, Toyoda Loom Works was on its way to record sales and profits.

Sakichi Toyoda was also an industrial philosopher who contemplated the individual's contribution to the company and the company's contribution to the larger world. He was fascinated by the work of other industrialists of the period, particularly Westerners. He found Smiles's work useful because it was based on a multitude of case studies that showed how many inventors and industrialists changed the course of society by blending ingenuity with a focus on bettering humankind through the workplace. Smiles showed how, by learning to be more efficient on the job, employees could improve the quality of their own lives and those of their coworkers. They also could improve the quality of life for the people who used the products they made, which were consequently of more use and value.

Said to be "a practical and engaging tribute" to workers, Smiles's book "awakens readers to their own potential, instills the desire to succeed, and helps people to apply themselves diligently to the right pursuits—sparing neither labor, pains, nor self-denial in prosecuting them—and to rely upon their own efforts in life." Essentially, it is a testament to the age-old proverb that good things come to those who help themselves. Smiles recommends ". . . that youth must work in order to enjoy; that nothing creditable can be accomplished without application and diligence; that the student must not be daunted by difficulties, but conquer them by patience and perseverance; and that, above all, he must seek elevation of character, without which capacity is worthless and worldly success is naught."

Such thoughts in regard to man and enterprise echoes a statement made during the same period by the Russian novelist and philosopher Leo Tolstoy, who said, "Everyone thinks of changing the world, but no one thinks of changing himself." Advances in machinery were occurring faster than most people could keep up with, but some leaders were beginning to recognize that automation without a foundation of human intelligence, if not compassion, would lead to a cold and less proficient world. For people to excel in the modern workplace, they would need to be effective thinkers who understood their ability to contribute both to themselves and to the larger community through daily work.

Inspired by Smiles, Sakichi Toyoda sought to make his contribution to altering the course of man, applying principles of humanity to his inventions. The result was the foundation for what would become one of the most effective corporations in the world. Until his death in 1930, he spent considerable time teaching his son, Kiichiro Toyoda (1894–1952), his philosophies about contributive business.

By the late 1920s, Sakichi Toyoda's loom company and dozens of patented inventions had established him as one of the twentieth century's most important figures in business. Still, he was far from satisfied, believing people's ability to solve problems is unlimited as long as they are willing to learn and explore. Toyoda believed engineers develop better products by learning firsthand in the factory instead of sitting behind a desk.

Therefore, when Kiichiro Toyoda went to work at Toyoda Loom Works after graduating from the university in Tokyo, his father urged him to experience the business from the ground up. Sakichi Toyoda also believed that observation of loom makers outside Japan was essential to making the factory globally competitive. He wanted his son to follow in his innovative footsteps by seeing, learning, and developing his own solutions to problems.

Sakichi Toyoda died in 1930, leaving Toyoda Automatic Loom Works to his son. Five years later, Kiichiro Toyoda honored his father by officially establishing Sakichi Toyoda's business philosophy as the operating principles of the company. These principles, or precepts, became the basis of what would later emerge as Toyota's specialized way of doing business.

THE ORIGINAL TOYODA PRECEPTS (1935)

1. Be contributive to the development and welfare of the country by working together, regardless of position, in faithfully fulfilling your duties.

2. Be ahead of the times through endless creativity, inquisitiveness, and pursuit of improvement.

3. Be practical and avoid frivolity.

4. Be kind and generous; strive to create a warm, homelike atmosphere.

5. Be reverent, and show gratitude for things great and small in thought and deed.

Conquer New Territory

At his father's urging, Kiichiro Toyoda traveled to Europe, further studying Platt Brothers' progress, and to Detroit in the United States, where he became fascinated with the American industrial movement, and automobiles in particular. He found Henry Ford's thriving empire—where assembly-line production made affordable cars for the masses—especially interesting and closely studied the company's efficient production process.

Kiichiro Toyoda found the American open roads alluring and recognized the opportunity given to citizens able to purchase affordable automobiles. In 1923, Japan had suffered a massive earthquake, which caused significant damage to the rail lines that made up the country's transportation infrastructure. Without access to trains, travel was difficult for most citizens in Japan. Toyoda recognized that if he could duplicate and improve upon American automobile design and production in Japan, just as his father had done with the weaving loom, he could provide affordable vehicles that would make long-distance transportation viable for all citizens.

So, in the late 1920s, when Platt Brothers offered to buy Sakichi Toyoda's patents from Toyoda Automatic Loom Works, Sakichi and Kiichiro Toyoda agreed. The sale gave Kiichiro one million yen—the equivalent of more than $20 million in today's currency—to finance the exploratory development of a Japanese automobile. It didn't matter that Loom Works' fortune had been made from the weaving equipment or that Japan had no expertise in high-level machine design and manufacturing; in developing an automobile, the Toyodas saw an opportunity to pursue one of Sakichi Toyoda's business ideals: the betterment of people through creative enterprise.

Working in a shop inside the loom factory with a small team of employees who had no previous automobile design experience, Kiichiro Toyoda produced the company's first automotive prototype in 1935. The AA went into production in 1936. It had the body shape of a Chrysler (with a few refinements like a more aerodynamic and stylish rounded form) and the engine of a Chevrolet, Japan's most popular car and therefore the one with the most readily available replacement parts.

Coinciding with the launch of its first car, Toyoda Automatic Loom Works held a competition to find a name and logo for its new automotive enterprise. Thousands of people responded. The company decided to replace the "d" in Toyoda with a "t" because the number of strokes needed to write "Toyota" in Japanese (eight) was thought to bring good luck and because the word "Toyota" looked and sounded more appealing and sleek, and therefore more automobile worthy. A Chinese language character emblem was chosen for the new Toyota logo. In 1937, Toyota Motor Company, Ltd., was established as a Japanese corporation in a rural area in Japan's Aichi prefecture located approximately 30 minutes outside of Nagoya (the location was later named Toyota City).

Toyota's first vehicles had numerous quality issues. The initial manufacturing process was rudimentary at best and was hardly competitive on a global scale. The first products were little more than modified knockoffs of Chrysler, Ford, and General Motors vehicles, but Kiichiro Toyoda was intent from the start on providing value. The first Toyota cars were more than 10 percent less expensive than their American counterparts.

During its first seven years in the auto business, Toyota produced only about 1,500 cars, instead finding its success in the truck market. The release of the company's first vehicles coincided with a new mandate from the Japanese government that required all automakers selling vehicles in the country to be majority-owned and -controlled by Japanese citizens, essentially halting U.S. imports. With reduced competition, Toyota's automotive operations continued to grow moderately until the commencement of World War II, which required the company to focus its efforts on military production.

Almost immediately after the war ended, the company as the world knows it today quickly began to emerge, built around Toyota's unique spirit of "making things" with an emphasis on cost-effective and employee input. In 1945, the United States government allowed Toyota to begin peacetime vehicle production in occupied Japan. The company was even allowed to participate in the American War Department's industrial training program, which focused on process improvement and employee development—areas that would become the company's cornerstone strengths.

In 1947 Toyota began selling the Model SA, known by the trade name Toyopet—its first affordable car for the masses. While it wasn't the most powerful or graceful of cars, the Toyopet was designed to be low-priced, rugged, and able to handle Japan's bumpy postwar roads. Customers responded enthusiastically, and the company produced its 100,000th vehicle that same year.

However, Toyota struggled mightily in 1950 under the weight of a Japanese economic recession that forced the company to lay off employees amid financial losses. Fortunately, a historic restructured labor agreement was reached at the same time management realized that the company needed to dramatically improve its operating procedures in order to survive long term. The company has not lost money since.

Toyota first arrived in the United States in the late 1950s after three employees were sent on a "go and see" mission and determined that the company should try its hand at sales in the foreign country. One small dealership was set up in Southern California to sell the imported Toyopet Crown, Toyota's flagship product in its home country. Promotion included ads that proclaimed, "Toyopet is your pet!" The cars, along with a couple of truck models, sold dismally for years until the company decided to make a more substantial commitment to the U.S. market. That's when it began to produce cars specifically designed for the American market, products like the 1965 Corona. In the 1980s Toyota started to build American manufacturing plants, like the one in Georgetown, Kentucky, while also investing heavily in American communities. All of these tactics would become key to the corporation's future growth, leading to operations in almost 30 countries, products sold in more than 170 countries and markets around the world, and results that would become the envy of the entire industry.

Commit to What Matters Most

Over the last quarter century, Toyota has never wavered from its core founding principles of respecting people and striving for continuous improvement. The basis for these principles derives both from aspects of Japanese culture and from the Western business philosophies adopted by Sakichi and Kiichiro Toyoda.

That is why Jim Press, president of Toyota Motor North America and one of the first Americans to join the company's close-knit inner circle of executives, scoffs at any suggestion that the company is anything today but a global enterprise driven by ideals culled over time from different cultures and philosophies. Yes, Toyota is a company founded and based in Japan, and yes, its Asian roots and heritage still play an integral role in its culture and methods of conducting business. That, however, is just a part of the equation, Press says, not the solitary reason for its success.

Time spent at any of Toyota's three headquarters buildings in Japan (the corporation does not distinguish a single building as its "global headquarters") reveals that the company is certainly very Japanese; the English language is scarce, as are foreigners. However, the business taking place inside is uniquely Toyota. Consider how two other major Japanese automakers, Mazda and Nissan, have both struggled over the past 20 years.

In the late 1990s, Nissan was all but bankrupt, and Mazda, now majority-controlled by Ford, has long struggled with a disjointed product line and inconsistent quality. Both are relatively solid companies, with many viable products; however, at one time or another both have faced the same thorny issues that have historically plagued America's Big Three automakers and many other global companies around the world.

The difference, says Jim Press, who left Ford to join Toyota in 1970, starts with attitude and approach: "The people in this company are more selfless. They have less ego and less 'I'm in it for me.'"

The first non-Japanese to lead Toyota Motor North America and to be named to Toyota Motor Corporation's board of directors, Press is credited with directly influencing the development of such popular products as the Tacoma and Camry and is widely considered one of the most effective and influential leaders in the automotive industry today. Nissan's Carlos Ghosn and General Motors' Bob Lutz get the headlines, one observer says, while General Motors' Rick Wagoner gets the anguish, but Toyota's Jim Press gets the results. However, in Toyota tradition, Press is the last person to speak of his own success. He refuses to respond to any comments made about his personal achievements.

A daily swimmer who, for 14 years in his early days working for Toyota in Southern California, lived with a wife and children on a 42-foot boat docked near the office ("We fished for our own food, our pets were ducks, and we did a lot of different water sports for activities"), Press is a nondrinker who consumes a high quantity of diet soda. He is generally regarded as a soft-spoken executive with a coaching leadership style. He talks with a slow, relaxed cadence and has been repeatedly called a "thoughtful, humble leader," yet has a way of moving others to action. He typifies what the company embodies most, which, as one Japanese employee described it, is "action, action, action."

One national publication called Press something of a loner, but that perhaps reflects his low-key profile in the automotive industry. He's not the flashy, "look at me, look at what I've done" leader who spends his time lavishly entertaining friends or associates or living beyond his means. During one interview, he politely excused himself after receiving a note passed from a colleague. It turned out a longtime friend who was not expected to live through the holidays had called to say he was doing better. Press apologized numerous times when he returned, saying the call was not only important, but personally imperative.

Jim Press is a Kansas native who grew up in a small town with an uncle who was a car dealer and a brother who was a car buff. He talks of loving cars from his earliest memory. He learned how to take apart go-kart engines and put them back together again. He ordered a go-kart kit from an ad in a magazine, assembled it alone, and started racing it.

As a teenager, Press worked as a car washer at his uncle's Chevrolet dealership and tinkered with engines and used cars on the side, finding his calling in internal combustion. At the age of sixteen, he drag-raced a 1955 Chevy ("It had a huge motor, six carburetors") and still professes to be a mechanic—nothing more, nothing less. Says Press: "The only class I got a good grade in was auto shop. I went to all of the car shows that came into the area and would take the programs and cut out all of the pictures to keep." Today, he drives a Camry hybrid, perfect for his new residence in Manhattan, New York. On most days, he walks to the office, leaving the car at home.

When Press had the chance to leave Ford Motor Company more than three decades ago, the move seemed to make little sense. However, there were so many layers of management at Ford that Press says while he was working for the company, he was totally removed from its leader, Henry Ford II. He saw Mr. Ford once, maybe, and that was in passing. Directives at Ford were passed down from one level of the ladder to the next, and one had to hope the translation, by the time it reached the bottom rung, was accurate. At Toyota, Press was working for the company's president and chairman from day one, even though in the beginning he was just a middle manager.

"I knew [Toyota's] cars were of good quality," says Press, on making the move from Ford, "and once I got in the door, everything just clicked. I could see the results of [the] work, see how everything fit together. It was very stimulating . . . it felt like home." As an employee at Ford, he recalls, he was once sent to a Thunderbird assembly plant to "see if I could find one they could ship that did not have vibrations." He told me he cringed when acquaintances asked where he worked because he knew it would invariably end up in a complaint about their car.

Press today represents everything Toyota stands for. While he is one of the more powerful executives in the global automotive business, he understands that he is no bigger than the entity, just one employee making his own contribution to a far bigger cause.

Press notes frequently, in fact, that his contribution to Toyota is no greater than that of an entry-level employee—despite the fact that he has immeasurable influence over the United States car market and has directly affected the lives of millions of Americans. He has done this by pushing Toyota's leadership to build such vehicles as the Tacoma and to bring the Prius to the country before its planned introduction. He attributes such insight to feedback from customers and dealers in the field. He won't carry one of Toyota's clear laminate business cards because the style doesn't allow him to write notes on the back for customers he encounters on the job. Before executive demands forced him to stop, Press used to carry a card that said, in essence, "If you or anyone you know has had trouble with a Toyota, call me."

Press flies to Japan several times a year to report to board members, engineers, and designers about what vehicles are needed to best serve the American consumer. The fact that a small-town Kansas native who joined the Japanese-based company as a lower-level manager has risen to sit on the board of directors is an incredible feat. The accomplishment is all the more impressive when one considers that, as of this writing, the company is expected to gross almost $200 billion in sales in 2007, with an industry-leading operating margin of more than 9 percent (triple the industry average). By any measure, this is clearly someone who lives up to the company's ideals.

Most notably, Jim Press is known for his personal habits and self-discipline. For example, he continually strives to improve his swimming strokes, despite having spent thousands of hours in the water over four decades. He also works hard to make sure his escalating company power does not compromise his view and appreciation of all employees. Simply, he excels not because of his ambition, but because he continually seeks self-improvement that benefits him and others. Thousands of Toyota employees doing the same has resulted in a world-class company with years of record results and promising growth in its future.

Be Willing to Improve

Toyota places so much emphasis on its employees' acceptance of the company's primary principles that getting a job at the company is an accomplishment in itself. To be considered for employment, one must subscribe to the belief that anything, from a loom to an automobile and the processes used to make them, can be improved, and that humans have the capacity to do so when they apply their efforts to the proper pursuits. Such talk would sound like mere public relations spin were it not entirely true.

Says Jim Press about Toyota's method of making things: "Over time, through a lot of hard work, we have evolved a complex system that works, most of the time. [Toyota] is kind of like a country, but it is not geographically comprised; it is not comprised of earth, but of people and processes that are between cultures—sort of a society within itself."

With a philosophy based on serving people, including its employees, its customers, and the wider public, Toyota's corporate structure is allowed to grow and change in support of its service-oriented goals. The company would probably be successful in any industry, since its secret is not so much how it builds things but how it approaches the process and mind-set of building things.

2

||||||||||||||||||

Strive for Continuous Improvement

Something is wrong if workers do not look around each day, find things that are tedious or boring, and then rewrite the procedures. Even last month's manual should be out of date.

—Taiichi Ohno, former Toyota executive vice president, key player in the development of Toyota's signature manufacturing system, TPS

GOOD CAN ALWAYS BE BETTER. Even great can be greater.

Based on this premise, scores of manufacturing and service companies, from General Motors to John Deere to Wal-Mart, have studied and implemented parts of Toyota's patented method of manufacturing, known as the Toyota Production System (TPS). This method aims to improve product quality and profitability through creative employee contributions. Also a signature formula for lean production, in which waste is minimized and efficiency maximized, TPS is widely viewed as Toyota's distinct advantage in the competitive global marketplace. At the heart of TPS are standardized processes that encourage individual contribution to unified goals and objectives.

TPS is not the single reason for Toyota's success, nor is it merely a collection of workplace tools and processes. However, nobody familiar with the company will deny that TPS is a very important piece of the corporation's singular success. Based on Toyota's decades-long commitment to *kaizen,* or the daily and ongoing process of continuous improvement through the elimination of waste (*muda*) in the workplace, TPS has become essential to Toyota and other companies throughout the globe. TPS is a guiding light for everyone from top-level executives to entry-level employees. It is arguably the most studied and emulated corporate philosophy and practice in modern business history. What company, after all, does not want continuous improvement?

There is a distinct difference between approaching TPS as a mere manufacturing tool and using it as a guiding principle by which to live and work. Yes, Toyota contributed significantly to the evolvement of lean production, and yes, the process began in assembly plants and remains rooted in the production process. However, the very nature of TPS embodies evolution. To be effectively applied in the twenty-first century, the *kaizen* principle must go beyond business-textbook jargon and assembly-line management. That is why some companies that apply lean production in manufacturing plants while conducting "business as usual" in other aspects of their company's operations are destined to achieve mediocre results at best.

Toyota competitor General Motors is a prime example. Throughout the 1980s and 1990s, GM integrated aspects of lean production and TPS into its manufacturing process. Some aspects took hold while others did not, but the adoption of lean production initiatives led to considerable progress in production efficiency, not only at GM, but at Ford and Chrysler as well. Despite these improvements, Toyota is leaving its competitors further and further behind, with unparalleled growth, sustainable profits, and consistent customer satisfaction. So, what's the difference?

Observe any Toyota facility for more than a few minutes and the answer becomes crystal clear. At Toyota, continuous improvement is not just a manufacturing plant initiative; it's a priority for thousands of individuals working in different areas and disciplines who share and subscribe to the same corporate goals. Sit in a company lunchroom in Japan and one hears employees talking about how they *"kaizened,"* or improved, an office policy; stand at any spot on any plant floor and ask someone to point out some physical results of *kaizen.* The number of examples one will hear will be overwhelming.

TPS is a collection of manufacturing methods
that incorporate three key philosophies:

- Customer first
- Employee satisfaction
- Company stability

Bigger Is Not Necessarily Better

General Motors, Ford, Chrysler, and other large automotive manufacturers are making better vehicles than ever before, due in large part to their adoption of lean production methods. However, over the past few decades these companies have become like overweight adults—outward in girth but not upward in stature. For more than 70 years, Michigan-based General

Motors has been the biggest automaker in the world, yet rarely in recent memory has it been called a great company.

As far back as anyone can remember, GM, in its role as industry juggernaut, was setting the labor terms for America's automakers, ignoring virtues like thrift and reasonability. GM would sign overtly generous contracts with the United Auto Workers (UAW) union, forcing Ford and Chrysler to follow suit. The company led the way on pricing and operated under the general presumption that nothing much mattered as long as GM was on top. In recent years, despite improvements made in its manufacturing processes, not much has changed at GM. In early 2007, for instance, GM chairman and chief executive officer Rick Wagoner publicly stated that largeness was indeed a company priority: "I like being No. 1," he said, "and I think our people take pride in that, so it's not something that we're going to sit back and let somebody else pass us by."

At General Motors and Ford, the view has long been that bigger is better. That mind-set was one Gary Convis wanted to escape, and he found sanctuary at Toyota.

Recognized as one of the world's foremost authorities on lean production, Convis became a member of Toyota Motor Corporation's inner management circle and an executive vice president of Toyota Motor Engineering & Manufacturing North America, Inc. He was a Ford employee for 18 years before taking a job with Toyota in 1984 as plant manager at New United Motor Manufacturing, Inc. (NUMMI; pronounced *new-me*), a joint venture between Toyota and General Motors. A Michigan native who graduated from Michigan State University, Convis also worked for GM early in his career. He was about as American-and-Detroit-autocentric as any automotive manager in the industry before he arrived at Toyota.

As the youngest-ever assistant plant manager in Ford's history, Convis worked out of a spacious corner office and drove an expensive company car. However, he turned it all in to join Toyota's ranks, even though that job came with a beat-up rental car, no private parking spot, and no private office. In the early 1980s, Toyota had no infrastructure in the United States, having never built a single car on American soil. The company was mostly known for its value-priced compact cars, while the U.S. carmakers were known for their upscale, luxury sedans.

Convis left Ford because he says he could "feel the world shrinking." He looked around and saw that America's largest automakers were "on thin ice" because they were not adapting to seismic shifts taking place in the marketplace. At Ford, for the most part, products were designed, built, and sold the same way they were years earlier. It was big, bureaucratic, and slow to adapt. When Convis was offered the opportunity to learn TPS at the NUMMI joint venture, he jumped at the chance. "My mom and dad thought I was crazy," says Convis. "I had no support."

The day after starting work at NUMMI, he boarded a plane for Japan to tour Toyota's Takaoka plant and see TPS in action. At both Ford and GM, Convis had heard about Toyota's superior manufacturing methods; seeing them, however, made him a believer. Says Convis, "To me, it was like looking at a symphony. Everybody knew their instrument and their music. They knew when to come in and when not to come in."

At NUMMI, Toyota's management team took the lead over GM's in manufacturing decisions and implementation because its methods were proven to be more efficient; this was precisely the reason General Motors wanted in on the partnership in the first place. The American automaker wanted to learn the finer points of lean production from the manufacturer that invented it, hoping that it would upgrade and improve its own production processes. For Toyota, NUMMI served as its first exposure to American workers, a kind of litmus test to see if American carmakers could build vehicles as effectively as Toyota did in Japan. As the general plant manager, Convis was able to learn from some of the world's best implementers of TPS.

The Fremont, California, NUMMI facility was transformed from a dinosaur into a thriving automotive assembly site. What Convis learned transcended wrenches and vehicle body components; what he learned was as much values and mind-set as it was methodology. All NUMMI employees ate together in one cafeteria, no managers had offices, and everyone wore the same uniform to work. More important, perhaps, was the fact that the Japanese charged with instilling TPS at NUMMI were not bosses but teachers (*sensei*) who passionately adhered to the company's principles of respect for people and continuous improvement. They constantly challenged the plant's employees, urging them to find more and better solutions, even when production seemed to be working well enough. And they were not afraid to get on the shop floor, if necessary, to see and learn firsthand in their never-ending quest for improvement. The lessons Convis learned on the job helped him to think differently about the duties and roles of effective leaders and employees.

"You don't cut corners," he says. "Not at any level."

Convis's statement sums up TPS and explains why it works in some instances and not in others. When it's only partially implemented, lean production is merely a tool, a lower-cost method for making products. At Toyota, however, lean production began as an extension of the company's basic founding principles, such as respect, thrift, and perseverance. It was practiced right from the start by employees at all levels, from plant workers to managers and executives, because it was part of the company's culture. Experts often say that TPS is Toyota's "unique approach to manufacturing." This is true, but in reality TPS is Toyota's unique approach to business as a whole. Improved production is the result, but *kaizen* also belongs in offices, as does almost every other element of TPS. Defining TPS implementation as nothing more than a production process misses a significant portion of the Toyota success story.

"The factory is the most visible and the easiest place to identify [TPS] at work," says Jim Press, "but the elements and the essence behind those principles are everywhere . . . from the service department at a Lexus dealership to the security man on premises [at Toyota Motor Sales USA in Torrance, California]."

Objectives of TPS:

- Highest quality
- Lowest cost
- Shortest lead time

Understand the Evolving System

Understanding how to benefit from the principles of Toyota's lean production system requires knowledge of both the creation and evolution of TPS. Most of the many books documenting the origins of TPS designate former Toyota executive vice president Taiichi Ohno as its creator. Ohno certainly played a significant, if not the leading role in the creation of

TPS, but he certainly did not do it alone. While Ohno is a key player in the developmental history of TPS (we will revisit Ohno's contributions later in this chapter), Toyota's system dates as far back as Sakichi and Kiichiro Toyoda and continues to develop today as company workers around the world find ways to change and refine it. Like the principle it supports—continuous improvement—TPS is designed as a fluid process fueled by employee contribution and creativity; rather than a set way of building things, it is a guide to finding continually better ways to build things.

Like his father, Kiichiro Toyoda had a desire to observe and learn that was insatiable. After establishing Toyota's automotive operations in 1936, he returned to the Detroit, Michigan, area to further study the American automotive industry. Most of his time was spent at the Ford Motor Company, which cooperated with him on his fact-finding mission. Toyoda read Henry Ford's then-popular book *Today and Tomorrow*, first published in 1926, gleaning inspiration from the principles of the Ford lean production system just as his father had found guidance in Samuel Smiles's *Self-Help*.

When Kiichiro Toyoda returned to Japan, he adapted Ford's system to Toyota's smaller production lines, changing assembly sequences and setting up a supplier network that provided production material as it was needed to avoid wasteful and expensive stockpiling. His adapted system was referred to inside Toyota as "just-in-time," meaning that materials would not arrive at the assembly line until absolutely necessary. Since money in the early days was extremely tight in Toyota's automotive operation, the company could hardly afford to stockpile expensive parts in the factory. Just-in-time provided a solution, allowing the company to use only what was needed.

The solution would evolve into one of the two core principles of TPS.

Toyota's signature manufacturing system continued to develop with the involvement of Eiji Toyoda, a nephew of Sakichi Toyoda who went to work for the company in 1936. In 1950, Eiji Toyoda also visited the Ford Motor Company in Detroit when he was named director of the Toyota Automotive Works. He returned to Japan intent on implementing the "suggestion system" he saw used effectively at Ford. Assembly-line workers there were encouraged to articulate their ideas for improvement, and Eiji Toyoda thought this system would work well at his company. The timeliness of this implementation of *kaizen* could not have been better; in 1950, Toyota was facing significant losses and massive layoffs and was in desperate need of new and better ways of working.

The formal employee contribution system gave workers a way to directly participate in decisions that made both their work conditions and the overall company better. It was based on the premise that the boss cannot see and know everything that workers are able to observe daily while doing their jobs. Asking employees for their ideas on an intermittent basis was not nearly as effective as instituting a formal policy that paid a cash reward if and when their suggestions were implemented.

With this system in place, Toyota was much more resilient during the company's next major crisis, the 1973 global oil shortage. Japan was hit hard by the shortage, during which consumer gasoline prices in the country rose almost 60 percent, in large part because the country imports almost 100 percent of its oil. Similarly, the cost of raw materials used by automakers rose roughly in direct proportion to the soaring oil and gas prices as suppliers tried to protect their own profit margins.

Sales dropped drastically at Toyota and at all of its competitors, including Nissan and Honda, by more than a third.

Prior to the shortage, Toyota employees had been suggesting an average of two to three improvements per employee each year. In 1973, the number increased to more than 10 per employee. Most concerned how Toyota could do more with less—cost-cutting ideas that would reduce capital expenditures. As a direct result, no employees were laid off and Toyota emerged from the crisis stronger than ever.

The suggestion system is used globally by Toyota today, in all divisions, and the total number of improvements made annually number in the hundreds of thousands. More than 600,000 suggestions were made in 2005 in Japan alone—an average of 11 per employee—and more than 99 percent were accepted. For each improvement made, employees receive cash bonuses ranging from 500 yen (about $5) to 200,000 yen (roughly $2,000).

Often, employee input focuses on little, seemingly trivial things, like adding a stool in an office to make retrieving records more efficient or rearranging tools on the manufacturing floor to make production easier. However, many suggestions implemented over the years, like the elevated mobile chairs or synchronized dollies used to maneuver in and around partially built vehicles on the assembly line, have dramatically changed Toyota's operations. All these improvements, both big and small, have added up significantly over the years to give Toyota a greater advantage.

Kaizen is the very first Japanese word that most new employees at U.S. Toyota facilities like those in San Antonio and Georgetown learn; it is the axis the company revolves around. Team members are not only encouraged but expected to con-

Eiji Toyoda's philosophy on what it takes to be a leader:

- Creativity
- Resourcefulness
- Wisdom
- Hard work

tribute to *kaizen*. Most companies set goals, then work to get there. While Toyota sets objectives too, its primary concern is simply getting better, every day, in every aspect of operations. One example: At Toyota Motor Manufacturing Kentucky (TMMK) in Georgetown, the convertible top on the Camry Solara used to take 30 minutes to install, but over time team members have *"kaizened"* it down to 8 minutes. If all goes according to plan at TMMK, the convertible-top installation time could be cut in half yet again within another few years. Stories of such improvement are told time and time again at Toyota, where the very idea of stagnant "business as usual" runs 180 degrees counter to the company's culture.

This is exactly the environment Taiichi Ohno hoped to inspire when he worked for decades to improve and personalize Toyota's manufacturing method. A graduate of Nagoya Technical High School in 1932 who went immediately to work

Effective *kaizen* relies on three principles:

- Process and results (not just results)
- Systematic thinking (seeing the big picture)
- Non-blaming (blame is wasteful)

at Toyoda Automatic Loom Works, Ohno moved over to Toyota Motor Co. and worked closely on just-in-time to improve Toyota's efficiency. He, too, read Henry Ford's book and studied the best principles of business at every opportunity.

Eiji Toyoda gave Ohno a directive to find ways to make Toyota more efficient, focusing particularly on materials efficiency since supplies were still scarce following the war. Toyota was in a difficult situation, not unlike what some U.S. automakers face today, and the company needed to significantly adapt and improve to survive. Ford was the global automotive industry leader at the time, but Ohno was not impressed by Ford's excessive inventory and its inefficiencies in workflow. Time, of course, would show that Ohno's assessment was correct. While once revolutionary, the Ford production system was flawed because it was not truly flexible or lean, nor did it empower workers to make improvements in the process. Executing the same tasks the same way every day leads to staleness and mediocrity. Ford's system became more dated and flawed simply because it stayed the same; there was no effort to ask employees how to do things more efficiently, and as a result, there was no such thing as continuous improvement.

By adding flexibility, giving factory workers decision-making authority, and improving both flow and efficiency at Toyota's manufacturing plants, Ohno in essence took the strengths of Ford's system and removed its weaknesses. The end product was Toyota's TPS, which reduced costs while raising quality—a powerful system.

Ohno was reportedly struck by the efficiencies of the U.S. grocery chain Piggly Wiggly during a later visit to America. By incorporating the American supermarket's practice of reordering and restocking goods only after customer purchases,

Toyota's lean production was made, well, more lean. Call it the Piggly Wiggly Way, and it had a big impact on Toyota, resulting in the company's "pull system" of production, which means that products are "pulled" from assembly by demand. At a company like General Motors, products are "pushed" onto customers. In other words, products are built according to how much the company hopes to sell rather than how much demand actually exists for those products.

At Toyota in Japan, vehicles are custom ordered—no product is built until it is ordered by a customer. Every car on the assembly line at a Toyota factory in Japan is on its way to a specific customer. In the United States, Toyota has to operate somewhat differently because car buyers tend to make on-the-spot purchases, but the company still maintains a modified pull system in which vehicles are not built unless dealers place specific orders for them.

GM, on the other hand, often has to offer deep discount incentives to prevent their inventory system from becoming entirely clogged. This is why Toyota's product turnaround in the United States averages about 30 days, while Ford and GM products turn over on average after 80 days or more, more than two and a half times slower than Toyota's.

With substantive input along the way from quality-control gurus like W. Edwards Deming, Joseph Duran, and Dr. Shigeo Shingo—Toyota's lead outside consultant and teacher—the company's production system was tweaked and significantly updated from about 1950 through the early 1970s. By the mid-1970s, while other Japanese automakers struggled, TPS had evolved enough to enable Toyota to avoid much of the pain from the cyclical downturn. Its refined system kept costs low and quality high. Recognizing the benefits of Toyota's lean production, other Japanese automakers, including Honda and Nissan, began implementing some of Toyota's techniques.

By the 1980s and 1990s, lean production and terms like *kaizen* emerged as buzzwords in global manufacturing. TPS was revered, studied, and copied throughout the world. It became so popular that many critics dismissed it as an overrated fad. Nonetheless, many American manufacturers implemented aspects of lean production and saw immediate improvements in both quality and cost. However, most companies made only piecemeal efforts at TPS implementation, applying it to just one plant or division rather than adopting it as a company-wide operating philosophy. The principles were applied mainly to production technique, and implementation was not always easy.

Many American companies have struggled with the system, says Steve Bera, a former GM employee and NUMMI manager who joined the California joint venture in its first days. He watched American plants try lean production in the 1980s and 1990s, only to be utterly disappointed. Facilities were set up to deliver parts to plants on a regular basis, inventories were minimized, and lean production was put into play. "But one thing was an Achilles heel," Bera says. "To play by those stringent and tight rules, every part must be perfect and quality [controlled] because there is no internal backup to support the organization if something goes wrong. Lean production is in place, but maybe suppliers don't have the same quality—a big problem. As soon as they started to see a failure, they would say, 'See, this lean system does not work.' Nobody knew how to mitigate the risk because they had never had to play by those rules."

Toyota, of course, continued improving its system, staying

several steps ahead while competitors began to develop their own TPS. The resulting lean enterprise is known inside Toyota today as the Toyota Way.

> TPS is built on two main principles:
>
> • Just-in-time—reducing wasteful inventory by using only "what is needed, when it is needed, and in the amount needed."
> • *Jidoka*—the ability to stop production lines by man or machine to ensure quality.

Implement at All Levels

TPS gains strength over time because it is based on trial and error. It fits well, therefore, with Toyota's founding principle of perseverance and hard work. Both the principles and practices at work in plants from Toyota City, Japan, to San Antonio, Texas, have been under constant development for decades. In theory, if a company does in fact continually improve, the system becomes self-sustaining, continually raising standards over time.

Kaizen, by its very nature, is not a quick-fix solution, nor is it a directive that can be barked out by a CEO hoping to achieve improvement in time for the next shareholders' meeting. That is why many people familiar with TPS and lean production who have been lured away from Toyota by other companies have been unable to achieve similar results. TPS is not a tool but a professional way of life that is bigger than management style. Some of Toyota's executives, for instance, have been un-usually effective—according to company results—yet many avid readers of the business pages have never heard of them. The system is bigger than the individual; even Gary Convis, considered one of the world's foremost authorities on lean production and Toyota's system, is quick to point out that it is much bigger than him.

"What we do," he says, "is not that simple."

A company cannot just hire Gary Convis and expect the organization to make an turnaround overnight, he says. Many experts even argue that, if implemented partially, hastily, and without respect for employees at all levels, *kaizen* results in *kaiaku*, or "change for the worse." An avid golfer, Convis relates the implementation of TPS to Tiger Woods's golf game: Anybody can go out and take lessons, but becoming another Tiger Woods is a difficult task. Tiger began working on his game as a child and has retooled his swing multiple times, even after winning golf's biggest events as a professional. Woods may be the best in the world, but he is always striving to get better, relentlessly chasing perfection in a game where perfection is not possible. Even an extraordinarily gifted golfer would have to put in years of practice and continuously improve his or her golf swing, attitude, and expectations to come close to approaching Tiger's prowess.

TPS is more like a lifestyle change than a crash diet. As a company, Toyota understands the pursuit of greatness as a long-term activity, resulting from the continual improvement of its processes. Toyota works toward tomorrow by getting better today.

"If you are going to be a leader at Toyota," says Convis, "you must always be working on day-to-day excellence."

Understanding how to implement TPS, with principles applicable to the largest manufacturing corporations as well as to small family businesses, begins with the understanding of

How to implement Toyota's *kaizen* culture in the workplace:

- Identify trouble
- Determine the root cause
- Develop a solution

exactly what it is: a system of regeneration, adaptation, and prosperity that increases quality while reducing waste by maximizing creative individual contributions.

Steven Spear and H. Kent Bowen stated once in a *Harvard Business Review* article that "one central tenet" of the company's corporate culture is responsible for just-in-time and Toyota's continuing success: "*ALL* work processes are controlled scientific experiments, constantly modified and improved by the people who do the work."

"People try to adapt parts of TPS, and they find it is not a panacea," says Dennis Cuneo, former Toyota Motor North America executive and current legal and site advisor for the company. "[TPS] is like software. It takes years to develop through patience and experience."

TPS is implemented on a daily basis by employees who eliminate waste, point out problems and system weaknesses, and make firsthand observations and recommendations for improvement. None of it works, however, without complete involvement on all levels. Consider a family trying to live on a budget in which one parent doesn't agree to cut back on spending. No matter how much the other family members save, that one person's uncontrolled expenditures will make it difficult for the rest of the family to meet their budget. Similarly, Toyota relies on its people to come together as working parts, from the plant floor to the president's office. TPS determines how products are made, but very same principles of *kaizen*, just-in-time, and *jidoka* are at work in offices and practiced by individuals around the world.

While the TPS principles are universal, they may take on slightly different forms outside the factory. The most prevalent nonmanufacturing application of TPS used in Toyota offices in Japan as well as America is a management practice first established by Walter Shewhart in his 1939 book *Statistical Methods from the Viewpoint of Quality Control*. The practice is an improvement cycle Shewhart identified as Plan-Do-Study-Act. In the 1950s, Shewhart's colleague W. Edwards Deming modified the term, renaming it the Plan-Do-Check-Act cycle. As previously noted, Deming influenced Toyota's management style as a consultant and also as one whose work was closely studied by Eiji Toyoda. Most of Deming's contributions occurred in the 1950s, when he traveled to Japan to assist in postwar economic recovery. Because the Japanese business community easily warmed to Deming's business theories, he was influential throughout the country, but he had the most impact at Toyota.

Deming's beliefs that higher quality leads to lower costs— ultimately providing more jobs and sustaining profits—and that companies should value social contributions over shareholder interests appealed to Toyota and integral members of the Toyota family. So did his modest lifestyle and lack of arrogance. His philosophies resonated with Toyota's culture and were consistent with the founding principles established by Sakichi and Kiichiro Toyoda.

In a way, Deming's theory of business was just a more systematic, refined, and functional approach to many of the same principles espoused years before by Samuel Smiles. The pieces, then, fit together beautifully. Toyota's leaders listened when Deming talked about production as a system rather than a sequence of unrelated events, and described standardization as an ever-rising upward spiral. The company still applies Deming's principles today.

"There is not a day I don't think about what Dr. Deming meant to us," said Shoichiro Toyoda, son of Kiichiro Toyoda and a Toyota director and honorary chairman. "Deming is the core of our management."

Some of Deming's ongoing contributions to Toyota are hard to quantify, such as commitment to quality and to people. Others are more specific and evident, such as his version of the improvement cycle, Plan-Do-Check-Act (PDCA). The PDCA principle is as vigorously at work at Toyota today as it was when it was first introduced. Most people in business follow only a sequence of Plan-Do, an abbreviated cycle in which someone decides what should be done and does it. According to the PDCA principle, if you continually work only in Plan-Do sequences, you never get a chance to appraise your mistakes and determine what isn't working. As a result, action is never taken to fix problems, and performance rarely improves.

By following the complete PDCA sequence, standards continually rise, providing a higher starting point for each cycle and yielding continual improvement. The result of PDCA is illustrated by a rising spiral, while those practicing just Plan-Do, who are unwilling or unable to check performance and take corrective action, spiral in circular motion in exactly the same spot, unable to move upward because they never raise their starting point.

Certainly Deming's business principles have been well-studied by many corporations around the world. Thousands of organizations have implemented various aspects of Deming's methods just as has Toyota. At Toyota, however, these practices are taken very seriously and have not been abandoned after years of practice. Quite frequently at meetings in Toyota offices from Tokyo to Toyota City, managers ask their employees, "Have you done your PDCA?"

Another way Toyota employees outside the plan setting strive for continual improvement is by producing what Toyota calls *horenso*. Derived from the Japanese words *hokoku* (giving a thorough update to somebody), *renraku* (staying in touch on a subject), and *soudan* (consultation about an issue), *horenso*—which sounds like the Japanese word for spinach—is a detailed progress report on issues or problems that is used for self-remembering purposes and for leaving a trail of explanation for coworkers and superiors.

Toyota has a strong cultural belief in work being interchangeable; according to this belief, if work is done well and properly, any employee trained in that area should be able to pick up where another left off, eliminating drops in quality and backward steps in day-to-day and year-to-year transitions. The company therefore spends a large amount of time training employees to write detailed reports—*horenso*—that explain an action so thoroughly that if the employee who wrote the report is absent one day and another employee needs to follow up on the issue in his or her absence, the information will be readily available and easy to comprehend. Thus another frequent saying around Toyota in Japan is "Did you remember your *horenso*?"

At many companies, *horenso* would be translated as simply copying superiors and fellow workers on e-mails so they are "in the loop," but in fact that is precisely the type of communication Toyota's *horenso* tries to overcome. Of course, Toyota employees copy one another on e-mails out of necessity, but that is not considered adequate communication. Continual improvement can only occur when thorough and clear consultation and communication take place. This standard of communication requires that responsible employees take the extra time to ensure that other employees have access to full and understandable explanations of their projects.

More Than a Formula

One of the keys to the success of Toyota's lean production and continuing improvement processes is that they are not formulaic to the point that they limit employee innovation. Instead, they are quite the opposite, serving as guides designed to unleash previously untapped employee potential. Deming believed, and Toyota's past and present leadership concurs, that principles should remain the same but methods for reaching objectives should constantly change: What works today can always be improved upon. Therefore, a central element of maintaining the same culture at Toyota year after year is encouraging employees to find different and new ways of contributing.

Many who study TPS or Toyota's way of working are often initially surprised at the lack of specific, step-by-step, how-to instructions. But the Toyota culture is intended to draw upon the creative abilities of employees; if the processes were put into a manual featuring steps 1, 2, and 3, then people would likely follow the steps robotically, doing their job each day precisely the same way they did it the day before.

"Ultimately," says Cuneo, "the Toyota system is teaching people to think [for] themselves and find a better way to do the job . . . to take individual ownership."

3

||||||||||||||||||

The Power of Humility

Once you buy into the system, you have to live the life, period.

—Gary Convis, senior executive adviser

for Toyota

PRINCIPLES DO NOT MEAN much when they are merely words on paper. Sure, leadership rhetoric might make sense and even serve as sage advice to those listening, but for real progress to occur over time leaders have to walk the talk, from the top of the organization down.

That is why one of Toyota's highest-ranking North American executives refuses a special parking place and walks through the assembly plant every day to reach his office. Such behavior by a top automotive industry executive is unusual, to say the least. Typically, one perk is piled onto another for car executives, from personal use of company jets to plush corner offices to chauffeurs and lavish expense accounts.

For those who know Gary Convis, however, his determination not to stand out from customers and other Toyota employees—even those on the shop floor—is not unusual at all. He not only preaches Toyota's unique way of doing business, he practices it every day—living the philosophy of respect for people.

During his first 16 years on the job with Toyota, Convis drove a Toyota Corolla, the company's best-selling compact car, to and from the office every day. He jokes that his neighbors, the ones who saw him driving around in a $15,000 compact, wouldn't believe he was an automotive executive; nor would visitors to Toyota's Georgetown, Kentucky, manufacturing plant once they realize that he has to grapple for first-come, first-served parking spots like everyone else. The lot is a quarter mile away from Convis's office, and since he is one of the leading manufacturing executives in the world, his time is of course invaluable. But then again, he says, so is everyone else's.

Convis maintains an office inside the Georgetown plant overlooking the manufacturing floor so he can remain accessible to all team members. He walks through the assembly plant daily so that hourly workers know he is in the trenches with them, trying to solve problems and make daily improvements to the way Toyota vehicles are built. Convis rarely takes advantage of the company plane because he regards it as excessive. Mostly, though, he tries not to distance himself from workers by displaying any hint of executive arrogance, which can be distracting, if not totally out of place.

"I have a deep sense of regard for our hourly team members," Convis says. "My job is to connect to them since they cannot easily come up and see me. When I wake up every morning I usually think about them first. . . . I think, people are at the plant already working trying to make improvements."

A golfer and Harley-Davidson enthusiast who lives in Lexington, Kentucky, with his wife and five children, Convis garners a lot of respect from his employees and others within the global automotive industry. He gets this respect not as a result of his position of authority but because of his knowledge, experience, and willingness to literally roll up his sleeves and assess problems. Says Convis: "You respect people. You listen to them, you work together."

On the manufacturing plant floor, Convis asks team members about assembly processes and finds inspiration in the dozens of improvement suggestions contributed by factory employees each month. "It's my favorite time of the day," he says. "It's where I grew up and that's where we add value. I like to say that the rest of us are all overhead. If I don't add value, there's no reason for me to be there."

How Toyota executive vice president Gary Convis lives the philosophy:

- Frequently flies coach, handling his own bags
- Eschews personal use of company jet
- Reads and manages his own e-mail
- Parks in the main plant employee lot: first-come, first-served
- Walks manufacturing facility floor daily
- Remains accessible to team members

Don't Give Others Reason to Doubt

Living the philosophy of one's company sounds so much like common sense that it should go without saying, but unfortunately this is rarely the case. In big business, people in high positions are tempted to take full advantage of perks and opportunities, no matter what the cost or how it looks to peers and fellow employees. They are the privileged in a working-class world, and being an executive has its benefits. One need only consider a story from the Ford Motor Company to understand the huge difference between the two companies.

Mark Fields, president of Ford's North American Automotive Division, was lambasted by the media for using more than $273,000 worth of personal flights on the company jet in one quarter of 2005 alone. If he kept up that rate of usage over the span of a year, the cost to the company would be more than $1 million. Of course, the flights were approved by corporate management and were explicitly included in the contract Fields signed when he was hired to restructure and save the struggling unit, which includes the flagship Ford Division of Ford Motor Company. Fields's family lives in Florida, and he commutes there and back from Detroit on weekends. Certainly for a man earning an average salary in the millions, an extra million in benefits might not seem like that big of a deal.

But Fields's chief responsibility is to rebuild Ford's North American automotive unit. The company as a whole is expected to lose close to $17 billion between the time Fields's flights were made public in 2005 and when Ford is projected to return to profitability, in 2009. The massive restructuring plan underway at Ford includes closing plants and eliminating thousands of jobs. Costs are being cut in almost every corner, and the new CEO Alan Mulally had to leverage the company's future by using its assets as collateral for a large loan to fund the turnaround plan. An extra $1 million in frivolous expenses by a top employee thus became a major issue to the other employees, some of whom vociferously objected to Fields's flights.

Some Ford employees went so far as to say that Fields's actions were inexcusable.

The disgruntled message got through to Fields, and he made amends by stopping personal flights on the company jet, announcing his decision to employees in an internal Webcast. The damage, however, had already been done. Leading a vitally important turnaround became much more difficult the moment news of the flight excess reached employees because Fields had shown he was not living the company philosophy.

Toyota's top executives, including president Katsuaki Watanabe, are also geographically challenged during the workweek, since the company operates from multiple headquarters in Japan, including Toyota City, Nagoya, and Tokyo. Watanabe has offices in each of the locations, as do other executives, and frequently he has to travel from Tokyo to the Nagoya and Toyota City areas for meetings. Even in Japan it is quite common for executives, especially those of leading car companies, to be chauffeured by automobile over longer distances. But typically, Watanabe and the members of his executive board can be found inconspicuously seated among the general public making the trips back and forth on the *Shinkansen* (public bullet train). Toyota executives don't follow suit, said one company employee, simply because Japan's trains are the most efficient means of transportation, and the company is all about efficiency. The company was adamant about placing its new Nagoya headquarters facility directly adjacent to the train station for this reason.

Toyota's Jim Press is about as comfortable talking about competitors is he is talking about himself—which is to say, not at all. While he will not address specifics of frivolous spending in the automotive industry, he will say on the record that the wasteful nature of executives at many big global corporations is completely puzzling to him. He added that it would not be acceptable within Toyota's culture, which abhors waste. When asked about executive salaries escalating well into the millions and lavish corporate perks that cost customers and shareholders a fortune, Press provides a simple response:

"Why?" he says. "I don't understand."

One should not assume that Toyota executives don't enjoy perks—they do. Outside the company's building in Tokyo, one is struck by the frequent appearance of chauffeur-driven sedans rolling into the garage underneath, bringing executives to work. The glass-windowed building, modestly sized for a contemporary major corporate office building, has tiered floors filled with employees of different ranks, much as one finds at General Motors or Ford in America or at nearby Nissan in Japan.

Clearly, all employees do not enjoy equal privileges at Toyota. The typical workplace for managers and staff in Japan is made up of open, *obeya*-style offices where communication and observation is easy, while top-level executives have larger, private offices. Neither are chauffeur-driven cars in Tokyo unusual, though it should be noted that traffic jams in the congested city make getting from one point to another by car a huge challenge. Executives also often have access to corporate tickets to baseball games at the nearby Tokyo Dome.

The difference at Toyota, however, is that executive arrogance is largely absent. The atmosphere inside the building is one of focus and disciplined work, with little or no frivolity. Executives are known to work the longest hours of all the employees and shoulder a large burden of responsibility. Also, while executives are well paid, they are not given absurd salaries rivaling those of professional athletes, much less competitors—a policy that goes back to the company's founding precepts of humility, thrift, and respect.

It has long been typical in Japan for CEOs to make no more than 17 times the pay of hourly workers. However, with the higher salaries earned by leaders like Nissan's Carlos Ghosn—who, along with his nine top executives, earned an average of $2 million in 2006—there has been a shift toward a decidedly more Western pay scale. At Toyota, though, top executives earned an average of just over $500,000 in 2006, nothing close to what top managers make at other corporations around the world; meanwhile, the Japanese automaker outearns almost all of them.

In addition to an executive pay scale that is more closely linked to that of average workers, Toyota's culture does not chastise lower-ranking employees for bringing problems to their superiors. This is a far cry from the culture one finds at, say, GM, where one hourly worker confided that if he didn't show up at work for a month, it would be less of problem than if he suggested to a superior that a process or decision was hurting the company.

"We are all kind of at the same level," says Jim Press, referring to Toyota's employee structure. "If you looked at the spread, the distance between the newest person just hired at the company and [the chairman of the board] is not that great. If we wanted to just get rich, we would all go work somewhere else. That is not what we are about."

Press says one Toyota employee is considered just as important as another, regardless of paycheck size or length of title. Each employee, he says, contributes to the greater good of the company, and one role is no more meaningful than another. When Press worked Toyota's Torrance, California, offices, he shared his company-sponsored courtside tickets to a Los Angeles Lakers game with a multitude of employees, including longtime company security guard Bobby Patterson. Acquaintances for almost two decades, Press, who is soft-spoken and known for keeping to himself, and Patterson frequently visit on Press's way in and out of the office, occasionally discussing the company and its customers. When the opportunity arose for Press to take an associate to a Lakers basketball game, Patterson got the invitation.

"I learn from him," says Press. "He *is* the company. If Dr. [Shoichiro] Toyoda is the champion of what we are doing, Bobby in security is number two. My job is only to serve the people of the organization, and that includes him."

Humility, the quality of being modest and respectful, is unquestionably a trait of the Japanese people in both practice and purpose, and this is likely one reason why Toyota's culture has blended so well over the years with the principles first instilled by Sakichi Toyoda and influenced by Westerners like Smiles and Deming. At Toyota, though, it is more than an intrinsic humility; it is a deeper respect for people that Jim Press says characterizes the company.

At each step along the way, as Toyota has evolved into the world's most successful global automaker, a kind of understated presence has pervaded the company. Some who try to characterize the company refer to it as quiet and conservative, probably in part because of this characteristic, but many closely associated with the company say it is more a deep commitment to being respectful of others that colors the prevailing corporate personality.

Perhaps Toyota's geographical history also contributes to this culture of actions speaking louder than words. It may be hard to imagine now, given the company's incredible product line (think of the luxurious Lexus or the hybrid Prius), but Toyota remains today and has always been a small-town corporation at heart, keeping a close connection to the customers it serves. Toyota City, Japan, where Toyota has not only its roots but also its largest concentration of manufacturing plants and operations, may be large compared to some American small towns, but the community is considered suburban countryside in Japan. The area was rural until Toyota arrived, and a prevailing small-town attitude has remained over the years, contributing to a kind of "country" reputation for the corporation in comparison to more urban Japanese corporations like Honda and Nissan.

Toyota's founding family has also remained grounded, keeping humility and respect for others close to the core. Members of the Toyoda family are widely revered in Japan for their success and for the temperance and commitment to the community they have displayed over the years. The family—including fourth-generation scion, company employee, and likely one-day company president fifty-two-year-old Akio Toyoda—lives together in a compound, maintaining a close-knit, grounded household culture. And, even though Toyota is a publicly traded company (symbol: TM, NYSE), the Toyodas remain closely involved with the corporation, largely because they control more than 40 percent of the voting stock through a family trust. They have significant influence on both the ongoing culture and operation of the company, similar to the Ford family's involvement with Ford Motor Company in the United States.

Dr. Shoichiro Toyoda, for instance, made an appearance in 2006 in San Antonio, Texas, when Toyota opened its new truck plant. When asked if the family still maintains an active presence on the company's managing board, Jim Press quickly says, "Oh yes." Another Toyota executive says Dr. Toyoda "sits in on every meeting" and is "not passive" in terms of company direction whatsoever, serving as a guiding hand just one generation removed from the company's founder. It is said that several years ago, Dr. Toyoda wanted the company to get more involved in the housing industry in Japan, believing it could provide high-quality, affordable prefabricated houses to the masses, so Toyota put more emphasis into this area and today builds more than 4,000 homes in Japan each year.

In some respects, because of its close-knit nature and continuing involvement with one of the world's largest companies, the Toyoda family is as close to royalty as one can find in Japan. Careful attention has been paid to education and marriage lines within the family as well. Mrs. Hiroko Toyoda, the wife of Dr. Shoichiro Toyoda, for instance, is a Mitsui, one of the oldest and wealthiest families in global business, dating back to the 1600s in Japan.

Mrs. Toyoda also reflected the Toyoda/Toyota characteristic humility. Jim Press encountered her on the train one day following a meeting in Tokyo. They both got off at Nagoya station. In her eighties, Mrs. Toyoda was walking alone, pulling her own suitcase through a heavy rush-hour crowd. Press offered her a hand, but she politely declined, shrugging as if to say, "Why?"

Maintain Proper Perspective

Toyota spends more on research and development than its competitors, industry observers say, laying out more than $20 million a day for the future. However, one of the company's most important investments in tomorrow—its culture—costs, by comparison, almost nothing at all. Just a few decades ago, Toyota was a moderately sized company largely centered in Japan. Today, it operates all over the world with close to 300,000 employees, including subsidiary workers. In the face of such growth, maintaining the company's original culture, particularly its emphasis on mutual respect, is of the utmost importance to Toyota's leadership. To address this, in 2001 the company founded the Toyota Institute, a global training center based in Japan where key employees from all over the world come to learn about the attributes that make Toyota so uniquely Toyota.

Like other instructional facilities, such as Toyota's Global Production Centers, which teach TPS on several continents, the institute is so important to the company's future that it falls under the direct supervision of president Katsuaki Watanabe—the so-called mayor of Toyota's Cultureville. Also, executive vice president Mitsuo Kinoshita serves as "sheriff," making sure Toyota's unique qualities are passed along to future employees. But the man responsible for seeing that Toyota's culture pervades, the "deputy sheriff" of the institute, is Koki Konishi, the effervescent director who, when talking about the company's traits, exudes a passion rarely found in Japanese corporate offices.

Among Koki Konishi's primary responsibilities is to make sure Toyota's business principles are properly understood so they can be passed along. The heart of his lessons involves the spirit and mind-set unique to Toyota. If employees do not live the philosophy and believe the philosophy, which starts with respect for people, Toyota could end up developing the cancerous culture of blame that exists in so many companies across the globe.

In a work culture characterized by blame, excuses get in the way of openness and a willingness to learn. In the Toyota

Koki Konishi's recommendations for preserving Toyota's culture:

1) Maintain historical perspective. "When we start, we have to always look back. Everything is for the future but we have to look at what we have previously done."

2) Assess with global perspective. "What is happening in Australia? What is happening in America? How does it all work together?"

3) Rely on ethics. "We have to see the world and our actions not only as a business person but also as a human. What is the impact?"

system, employees are not simply told, "This is the way you do it"; they are encouraged to find solutions and improvements that benefit not only customers but also themselves. A company cannot thrive on the basis of its processes alone, says Konishi, if its employees do not start work with the right philosophical foundation.

4

Rid All That Adds No Value

A place for everything, and everything in its place.

—Samuel Smiles, author, *Self-Help*

IN BUSINESS, as in life, subtraction is almost always as powerful as addition. In some instances it's even more so. Imagine a hiker desperate to reach his final destination, still miles
away, by sundown. To get there, he has to pick up his pace considerably. He quickens his stride, but he still isn't moving fast
enough. His backpack is full of weighty food and supplies he
no longer needs. He stops, empties it, and resumes his hike
several pounds lighter. As a result, his pace increases, allowing
him to easily arrive on time.

Progress comes not just from moving forward, but from also
removing hindrances along the way. A world-class swimmer
adds a stroke but also removes body hair before a big meet; a

professional football player increases strength but also loses weight before a new season; a carpenter buys a new, more powerful saw but also learns to decrease the number of strokes needed to drive in nails.

At Toyota, employees are encouraged to be the hiker, the swimmer, the football player, and the carpenter every day. *Muda*, the Japanese word for waste, is a central component of Toyota's success in regard to its elimination. While many companies focus on adding steps to a job or initiatives to a solution, Toyota focuses on removing waste from all aspects of its business—from reducing the number of steps team members take on assembly-line floors, to eliminating excess inventory, to reducing the amount of extraneous packaging material in parts shipments.

Kiichiro Toyoda learned from his father, Sakichi Toyoda, that waste was the great inhibitor of both man and machine, and his creation of Toyota's just-in-time method was specifically aimed at fostering his belief that "the ideal conditions for making things are created when machines, facilities, and people work together to add value without generating any waste."

Like most of Toyota's core principles, the elimination of waste began on the factory floor, but over time it has become an important philosophy practiced at all levels of the company. Talk to Jim Press for a while and he'll mention the word "waste" numerous times. For Toyota's hourly team members the elimination of waste is the second most important task of the day, right behind showing up for work.

The bottom line at Toyota: **If a process or an activity does not add value, get rid of it.**

Reduce Clutter, Reduce Ills

Toyota's Motomachi assembly plant, located in Toyota City, has been building vehicles since 1959, when it opened as the first car-exclusive manufacturing facility in Asia. One of 12 Toyota plants located in the Toyota City metropolitan area, it is known for globally proficient automobile production. Making such vehicles for the Japanese market as Toyota's Crown and Estima, the Motomachi plant uses 4,800 Japanese workers to build 650 vehicles per day on one assembly line.

Outfitted with ultraflexible manufacturing that allows eight different made-to-order cars to be built in the sequence in which customers have prepurchased them, the plant is a testament to Toyota's pull-based production system. During one plant tour, the assistant plant manager asked a visitor if he had seen any of the equipment in use at Toyota at the plants of Toyota's competitors. When he received an affirmative answer, the manager smiled, responding through a translator, "Same equipment, yes; but we use it differently." By "differently," he meant as efficiently as possible.

For years, for instance, Toyota's lean production system required team members to gather a small pile of parts sufficient for the number of vehicles coming down the line. True to the company's low-inventory philosophy, the piles were few in number, but managers and team members realized the system could be improved upon even further. In 2007, they devised a system in which one worker gathered all the parts for a single vehicle on a mobile trolley and transferred them to the moving assembly line. The process eliminated wasteful confusion that could occur when multiple vehicles were being built at once, further organizing the process. Such waste elimination may seem small on an individual scale, but in the scheme of hundreds of thousands of vehicles being built around the world each year, it all adds up.

The manufacturing process itself may not be the most impressive sight in the plant, however. What visitors to Toyota's Motomachi plant see is the same thing that visitors to Toyota's Georgetown, Kentucky, plant see: the cleanest automotive manufacturing plant in the industry. Most up-to-date assembly plants, like Ford's Rouge truck assembly plant in Michigan, or Nissan's plant in Mississippi, are twenty-first-century marvels when it comes to the manufacturing process. They are flexible and massive at the same time, able to produce hundreds of thousands of high-quality vehicles. But nothing compares with the scenery found inside Toyota's plants. Technologically, everything appears equal with the competition; aesthetically, the competition is not even close. The reason has everything to do with the elimination of waste to support continuous improvement.

Toyota's largest manufacturing plant outside Japan—the Georgetown, Kentucky, facility—is large enough to engulf more than 150 football fields. Under the daily guidance of a former General Motors executive, Steve St. Angelo, the plant's objective is to reach the production, quality, and efficiency standards set by Toyota plants in Japan. In some areas it has a way to go, but the Georgetown plant, which makes the Camry and Avalon sedans, the Camry Solara two-door car, and the Camry hybrid, already operates at near zero waste in terms of raw materials.

With roughly 7,000 team members coming and going throughout the day and into the night, the assembly-line work space would seem to need a little upkeep by the end of a shift. But traversing the facility from end to end reveals a manufacturing plant more clean and orderly than most hospitals or homes, much less most automotive assembly plants. The concrete flooring is spotless, trash is nonexistent, and the only excess aside from crates holding parts is the occasional foosball table purchased by team members to play during their breaks.

The Georgetown plant's cleanliness, like that at other Toyota facilities, is a direct result of an admitted corporate obsession with the elimination of waste. Clutter is distracting and therefore has no place in the Toyota system. Add in the company's commitment to the environment, and the result is a near-spotless plant.

This order is not achieved by continual cleaners sweeping the facility at all hours, but through a process that expels waste along the way. More than 90 percent of the parts received by Toyota's Georgetown plant come in returnable, reusable packaging. When parts are used, empty containers are stacked up and returned on the next truck, to be loaded up again. If parts or specially ordered items are shipped to the plant in traditional cardboard and plastic packaging, immediate recycling is in order. Everything is broken down and put in proper bins. There is no waste; workers sort material into bins for recycling, reuse, or composting. The compost nourishes an on-site garden and greenhouse that produce vegetables for local food pantries and pumpkins for team members' children on Halloween.

Such conservational action is enough to elicit rare, bold talk from Toyota executives. Declares Jim Press: "Toyota is proud of its [environmental] accomplishments, but more importantly, we accept the challenge to become the best environmental company in the world."

With no waste, plant cleanliness is sustainable. Recycling at the Georgetown plant exceeds 100,000 tons per year—including more than 45,000 lightbulbs—and the plant has been a "zero landfill" nonhazardous waste facility for several years. All of Toyota's manufacturing facilities, in fact, are zero landfill.

Compare this with Ford's $2 billion Rouge plant, hailed for its innovative environmental approach. With the world's largest living roof and renewable energy sources like solar cells and fuel cells providing its power, the Rouge plant is the company's "good works" centerpiece. Rouge visitors are awed by the creativity and enormity of Ford's commitment and investment, but ironically, Rouge is not a zero landfill plant. For some years, the American automaker has been working with a "total waste management" approach in its facilities to reach zero landfill, but even the best facilities, like Ford's St. Thomas, Ontario, assembly plant, have reduced the amount of waste sent to landfills by only 50 percent.

Two of General Motors' plants reached zero landfill status by 2006—a notable accomplishment in the eyes of global environmentalists—but both were smaller engine plants, not large assembly plants.

Statistically, the differences in conservation may be minor, but consumers are paying attention. They have been far more responsive to Toyota's action in recent years than to Ford's talk, reinforcing the adage that if you do the right things in business, over time customers cannot help but notice.

Never Surrender to Never-Ending Waste

Removing waste might be one of the most significant challenges companies face. By its nature, addition in the corporate and business world is much easier than subtraction because it does not rely so heavily on the acceptance of team members.

To eliminate waste, however, team members must be willing to accept that the current way is not the best way. The natural human tendency is to reject change, even if it would allow a process or job to be done more effectively. That is why humility is such an important aspect of Toyota's corporate culture. Team members who are sure they are right all of the time get directly in the way of *kaizen*, impeding continuous improvement. To counter such resistance to change and correction, Toyota has not been shy about using videotape evidence to reveal worker waste in action.

Take an assembly-line welder as one example. Assume she is the most efficient welder in the entire factory. If a manager or peer tells her that her welding technique could be improved, she will likely reject the critique. "Who at this plant welds better than me?" she could say. But if a manager called this team member in for a quality briefing and showed videotape proving needless steps were being taken and job production could be sped up considerably, the welder in question would have to agree.

One former Georgetown employee who worked for years in quality control told me videotape was their most effective weapon in fighting waste. Yes, she said, some workers found the evidential critique intrusive, and yes, videotaping employees on the line is not something company officials particularly like to talk about publicly. However, she said, such fact-based assessment is one of the primary reasons the Georgetown facility was able to approach Toyota's Japanese manufacturing efficiency so quickly. Facts speak for themselves, so if you want to get rid of waste, you have to adequately expose it. Then, no matter where the facility is located—in Japan, the United States, Europe, or elsewhere in the world—continuous improvement through waste elimination becomes merely a matter of whether employees are humble enough to accept the critique and make the change.

Such a waste elimination proposition sounds simple enough, but for most companies that is hardly the case. In the United States, for example, many feel the United Auto Workers (UAW) union goes so far as to cover up ongoing waste in the workplace, a situation that has given Toyota a significant advantage in its rise to the top.

A General Motors employee who has been an hourly worker for more than 20 years says the union works well for "lazy" and "inefficient" employees because the system protects the wastefulness of members who come to work late or struggle with on-the-job tasks. Videotape surveillance wouldn't fly at a GM factory in Flint, Michigan, where management doesn't even have the ability to assess an employee's performance. Protocol dictates that employees must be managed internally by another UAW member. Without direct access to employees, managers at unionized facilities have little power to reduce waste on the assembly line. As a result, Toyota continues to gain competitive advantage with each passing year that it runs lighter and faster with less waste to weigh it down.

Those who have studied the Toyota Production System may be familiar with an aspect of the system widely known as the "seven types of waste." While Taiichi Ohno did divide waste into seven categories to explain TPS in simple teaching terms and help people understand what to look for, these seven categories are not formally instituted as part of the system itself. But because Toyota's system is broadly defined, leaving the details up to team members, teachers frequently have to give specifics to help explain it. Therefore, the seven types of waste were identified and have remained a part of

TPS in manufacturing for many years, serving mostly as a guide for understanding what to look for.

Seven types of waste (*muda*) identified in TPS by Taiichi Ohno, and remedies for their elimination:

1. Overproduction: Slow production of parts or products to only what is necessary or required by customers.
2. Waiting: Eliminate any idle time that can be used more productively.
3. Excess conveyance: Stop unnecessary transportation of parts and materials from one place to the next.
4. Overprocessing: Cease all actions that do not benefit the customer in any way.
5. Excess inventory: Maintain a "buy one, sell one" philosophy; keep on hand no more than is demanded by customers.
6. Unnecessary motion: Reduce movement by people and equipment that does not add value to the company or the customer.
7. Defects and corrections: Stop defects at the source, before going on to another step.

The problem with dividing waste into such specific categories is that employees may rely solely on these guidelines rather than look beyond them to identify other kinds of waste they might fail to address. Toyota's culture tries to fight such mental hurdles. As former executive Dennis Cuneo says, Toyota's foundation is "software, not hardware." The intention is to teach awareness and problem solving, not to dictate rigid guidelines that must be followed "or else." Therefore, the Toyota philosophy is simply to organize all jobs around human activity in the workplace, creating an efficient sequence called "standardized work."

In manufacturing, TPS relies on three components, including: (1) *takt* time—the time that should be taken to produce a component on one vehicle; (2) working sequence—the sequence of operations in a single process needed to make quality goods most efficiently; and (3) standard in-process stock—the minimum amount of parts inventory needed on hand to allow workers to continuously do their job without interruption. In offices, the system relies on essentially the same components, but with less technical jargon. The corporate aim is for employees of all disciplines and levels to strive to do more and better with only what is needed.

So, while the seven types of waste are used by some in teaching lean production, Toyota teaches internally that waste is not limited to seven types but is in fact infinite. Fortunately, from the company perspective, employees' ability to find and eliminate waste is infinite as well. According to Toyota's culture, the greatest waste is the underutilization of people.

Says Mitsuo Kinoshita, Toyota's executive vice president in charge of global human resources: "We believe that human beings should have infinite possibilities to explore. In the United States and Europe most employees have descriptions which are limiting. Employees are not encouraged to go beyond [them]. We have job descriptions, too, but for guidance. Employees are encouraged to go beyond [their job descriptions] and be creative. We want to create infinite possibilities."

Seek Value Innovation

When Katsuaki Watanabe was named president of Toyota Motor Corporation in 2005, some onlookers were surprised by the choice. Unlike most top executives, he was not from sales, finance, or manufacturing—the more visible if not glamorous areas of automotive operations. Watanabe's predecessor, Fujio Cho, was the president of Toyota's first American manufacturing plant and was well-known around the world for his easygoing, irresistible personality. Watanabe, on the other hand, was barely known outside Japan at the time of his appointment. He had previously served as executive vice president in charge of the less-than-romantic cost-cutting department.

Watanabe had been working at Toyota since he graduated from Japan's Keio University with a degree in economics in 1964. For many of his more than 40 years with the company, Watanabe didn't even work with cars. His first job was overseeing the company's cafeteria. With Toyota's focus on identifying and removing waste, Watanabe was a perfect fit for the company. As a young cafeteria manager, he polled workers on their favorite dishes, tracked servings, and maintained a notebook full of data revealing much waste, from excess inventory and defects to overproduction and underutilized employees.

"People thought it was strange that a guy was taking data in the kitchen," recalls Watanabe. "There was so much waste, so I saw there was clearly room for improvement."

Needless to say, he rose to Toyota's top ranks in large part because he champions what Toyota is all about—making continuous improvement through a low tolerance of waste. A classical music enthusiast who sang in his college's men's choir, Watanabe is generally soft-spoken and reserved but armed with wit and not afraid to use it. In an interview shortly after taking Toyota's top operational job, he was asked about identifying areas of excess and trimming fat at the company. He replied, "Look, there are two PR people right there."

Watanabe rose through Toyota's administrative ranks, working in purchasing, corporate planning, and administrative affairs. He became a member of the company's tightly knit board of directors in 1992. His greatest impact at Toyota, though, involves the massive elimination of waste in one of the most effective cost-cutting initiatives ever recorded at a global company. Dubbed CCC21—Construction of Cost Competitiveness for the 21st Century—the program was initiated in 2000 to prevent Toyota from losing its edge to competitors like Nissan, which had formed an alliance with Renault and promised to cut costs through joint purchasing and benchmarking, and DaimlerChrysler, which promised to do the same.

Led by Watanabe, CCC21, in just over five years, eliminated more than $10 billion in costs for Toyota through a multilayered process aimed both internally and at suppliers—a result even more striking than Carlos Ghosn's daring 1999 Nissan Revival Plan. Industry observers concur that for the most part Toyota was, amazingly, able to increase quality while drastically reducing costs. This double-edged accomplishment was achieved by working with suppliers and helping them find ways to reduce costs through waste elimination as opposed to a hard-line mandate of "get it out now, at any cost to the customer." By working closely with suppliers to help them find waste, Toyota cut costs mostly through process improvements, not reductions in materials or quality.

Earning himself the nickname "Mr. Kaizen" inside Toyota and prompting one leading business publication to suggest he was "a demon at spotting costs that no one even knew existed and eliminating redundancies that few had noticed," Watanabe found cuts where others never thought of looking. Some of it was logic—the recognition that if all Toyota vehicles used the same parts, the cost would come down. Some of it, however, ran far deeper. *Business Week,* in fact, reported in 2005 that under Watanabe's lead, "one Toyota CCC21 team disassembled the horns made by a Japanese supplier and found ways to eliminate six of 28 components, resulting in a 40% cost reduction," while 35 different interior assist grips used on car doors were whittled down to 3, resulting in substantial savings over time.

Improvements under CCC21 are one reason Toyota posted its highest-ever net profit in 2006—roughly $17 billion—and the company's market capitalization grew well beyond $200 billion at the same time competitors' profits and market capitalization were drastically shrinking. Now, Watanabe is leading Toyota in the second phase of its massive waste reduction plan. Named Value Innovation, the initiative aims to go much deeper than cutting costs of individual parts with suppliers by going back to the origin of product development. If Toyota improves its designs and the design process, and treats associated vehicle parts as integrated systems, Watanabe believes, fewer parts may be needed, production time will decrease, and consumers will again receive more quality for less.

5

||||||||||||||||||

Improve Quality by Exposing the Truth

The world-class quality we have built is our lifeline.

—Katsuaki Watanabe, president, Toyota Motor Corporation

WHETHER THEY ARE in manufacturing production or administrative processes, defects cannot be eliminated unless their causes are properly and thoroughly identified at the source. Talk about quality all you want, make it a core initiative in the company mission statement, post flyers about it throughout the office, and describe it to customers and shareholders as a top priority: Little will come from the effort as long as defects are allowed to travel unchecked through manufacturing or administration.

The same scenario plays out all over the business world each day. Companies claim quality is of the utmost importance to the firm, yet somehow a breakdown occurs between articulation and execution. The common result is a whole lot of lip service paid to products, service, and results that end up having the same me-too quality as one's competitors. For instance, Ford, the company that adopted the slogan "Quality Is Job One" in the 1970s and has placards touting quality posted liberally throughout its manufacturing facilities, received a lot of positive press for greatly reducing its vehicle recalls in 2006. While its total number of recalls in the United States still exceeded 1.7 million, placing Ford on par with General Motors, this was seen as a great improvement compared to the more than 6 million recalls from the year before.

Toyota, which was roughly the same size as Ford at the time, recalled less than half that number of vehicles in 2006. Still, company president Watanabe was so troubled by Toyota's imperfection figure that he bowed publicly in apology. When a company has led its competitors in most consumer quality rankings for the past 20 years and relies the way Toyota does on quality as a key differentiator, defects in any measurable quantity are not acceptable, even if the results easily best those of peers.

That is why Toyota's culture works aggressively to increase quality by identifying the root causes of defects, both in the factory and the office. Some results of this corporate near-obsession with problem-solving are easily measured. In manufacturing, J.D. Power and Associates' product quality studies have shown Toyota to be the industry leader for many years. Other results are more discreet but visible nonetheless, such as Toyota's profit and growth sustainability since the late 1980s, a period in which competitors' numbers have wildly fluctuated. Whether on the assembly floor or in office buildings, Toyota team members are taught from the earliest days of their employment to practice three core steps to ensure quality, protecting both the company's current positioning and future opportunities.

Toyota steps to quality:

1. Speak up immediately when problems are recognized, no matter what.
2. Ask why (at least five times), to reach the root cause.
3. Go to the source of the problem and see for yourself.

Pull the Cord (or Pay the Price)

Before problems can be fixed, they must be identified. The Toyota Production System is built around visual signals that allow team members to notify each other about everything from needs to problems found. Simple and clear communication is the key. Jim Press once proclaimed, "If there is a problem, stop the train; do not let it go an inch farther." That neatly sums up the Toyota approach to quality.

In manufacturing, the physical tool that links each assembly worker to the line and each Toyota line to another, whether in the United States, Japan, or elsewhere, is the andon cord. Originating from the Japanese word for "lamp," andons are lights attached to machines or production lines that indicate operation status. The andon cord connects to the lights and runs along both sides of the assembly line. When a team member pulls one of the draping cords, activating the lights, the entire line is automatically stopped so processes remain in coordination and the problem can be addressed. The message workers learn early on and find continually reinforced is that finding and pointing out problems is a good thing, even though it stops the process.

At many Toyota plants, like the one in Georgetown, Kentucky, andon cords are pulled up to 5,000 times a day for safety and quality reasons. At Toyota's many assembly plants throughout the world, someone is likely pulling an andon cord every few seconds. Stopping the line is certainly costly in the short term, a slowing of vital production time. At some companies, such a move would result in a superior warning, "This had better be good." The opposite is true at Toyota, though, where one of the only ways employees can get in trouble, says one company executive, is by *not* pulling the cord if a problem is spotted or suspected. So important is the andon cord and what it stands for in Toyota's system that using it properly is one of the primary points of being a good employee.

Essential demands of Toyota employees, according to Gary Convis:

1. Come to work every day.
2. Pull the cord when there's a problem.

Pulling the cord for quality control on the assembly line has led to Toyota's strong value reputation with consumers, but that alone is not what transformed Toyota from a formidable Japanese business into a global juggernaut. Like all of Toyota's core principles, what began as an assembly-line aspect of lean production (pulling the cord) evolved over time into a company-wide business culture in which ideals are both cross-functional and cross-level. Thus on the administrative side of the company, pulling the cord means the same thing it does on the manufacturing side—it alerts the team to problems immediately, no matter what.

People are not perfect, of course, and neither are companies. Toyota, despite its multiple strengths and pervasive pull-the-cord principle, is no exception. The company reached an all-time high for product recalls in 2005. It made headlines in 2006 when it settled a sexual harassment lawsuit against a top American official in which the plaintiff claimed to have filed a complaint internally and received no response. In the same year, Japanese authorities launched a criminal investigation of several Toyota officials suspected of failing to disclose a potentially faulty steering part in some vehicles; as a result, the company was formally reprimanded by the Japanese government.

In each of these instances, Toyota responded aggressively, publicly taking responsibility for quality lapses and recalls and imposing steps to improve the situation. In the case of the settled lawsuit, the company instituted new policies and procedures intended to make sure any employee reports of misconduct were investigated immediately and thoroughly. Such actions in response to quality problems make it clear Toyota aims for excellence. Having such an aspiration, however, is only the first step. The second step, the map for getting there, requires the adoption of processes and procedures like pulling the cord— literally and figuratively.

This principle of accountability is one Ford could have used as it spiraled out of control for three-quarters of a decade, losing its grip as one of the world's strongest companies and most respected brands. Many people close to the company during the leadership of former CEO Bill Ford Jr. report that Ford was making admirable progress in 2003, around the time of its 100th anniversary. Financials seemed to stabilize, vision seemed clearer, and the realities of the company's operations seemed to be more transparent and under closer scrutiny. With new products, like the restyled F-150 pickup, and seemingly proactive leadership, better days appeared to be ahead. Many observers in the business world were surprised in 2006 when Bill Ford talked publicly about needing to get honesty on the table from his team. While accepting the Automotive Industry Executive of the Year award in Detroit, Ford said that he could deal with anything except a lack of truth. He called for honest input from his team to help him make good decisions for the company.

The very notion that executives would not be forthcoming with the company's chairman, CEO, and namesake is difficult to imagine, but it apparently happened. The willing deception continued after the appointment of Alan Mulally, who left Boeing to become Ford's CEO. In meetings during Mulally's first weeks on the job, it was reported that, when presented with results and forecasts by department heads, Mulally found the numbers did not match up with emerging truths about Ford's increasingly woeful situation.

"Why don't all the pieces add up for the total corporate financials?" he reportedly asked.

"We don't share everything," one manager replied.

Mulally made immediate changes to Ford's executive reporting process, demanding real numbers in real time. The fact that he had to do so highlights the differences between Ford and Toyota in approach, company culture, and, ultimately, results. Such a lack of openness is one reason Ford has been struggling in recent years while Toyota has been marching toward the top. Among Toyota's inner circle of managing directors, the pressure to reveal the truth is pervasive. Ask members of the executive team about openness with one another in terms of Toyota's business, and it immediately becomes clear that hiding negative facts is not an option. Executives, says Gary Convis, challenge one another constantly, albeit in a congenial business style, striving to find the truth.

"It is always interesting," says Convis, smiling, "but not always comfortable."

At Toyota, no level of employee, not even an executive, is excused from employing fact-based decision making. If uninvestigated hearsay or partial truths are used as the basis for recommended action, employees are usually told to conduct a more thorough investigation. The idea is that business is difficult enough even with full understanding and disclosure; without it, sustainability becomes difficult, if not impossible. Thus, Toyota has several processes that are frequently used throughout the company to investigate and reach the root causes of problems to ensure quality.

Continually Ask Why (at Least Five Times)

Questions are gateways to truths.

They are also a thinking person's weapon, powerful in removing superficial layers that obscure reality and give competitors an edge. At Toyota, the interrogatory has been a primary means of investigating problems for decades, dating back to the early days of TPS. Taiichi Ohno frequently talked about reaching the root cause of problems through a technique originally employed by company engineers in product development. It involved asking questions to access ever deeper layers of truth and is known at Toyota as "the Five Whys."

The Five Whys is a simple but highly effective method for exposing manufacturing problems. Layered interrogation gets team members to think below the surface of a problem and consider the chain reaction of consequences that lead back to the originating source of trouble.

Former Toyota Motor Manufacturing North America, Inc., president and CEO Teruyuki Minoura, now retired, used to talk among employees and in public speeches about learning the values and methods of TPS from Ohno. Once, Minoura said, Ohno drew a circle on the floor in the middle of a congested area in a production facility and told him to stand in it for hours. Viewing the bustling activity immediately around him while standing in isolation forced Minoura to ask probing questions about what he had previously viewed as business as usual: Why does that worker walk eight steps when only four are needed? Why do parts arrive before the worker needs them?

Minoura got the point, and the story has become a legend of TPS lore, illustrating the importance of fact-finding through questioning. The belief is that one or two questions are not enough. However, repeating interrogatories through five levels of investigation usually reveals the true source of a problem— thus the technique's name. Toyota's five whys became notable in the 1970s after manufacturing managers and experts from around the world began studying the company's production methods. The technique has spread and evolved into well-known methods like Six Sigma (a Motorola-developed system for eliminating defects) and has found everyday applications in areas like parenting and small-business human resource management. The concept amounts to little more than a questioner naively and innocently asking "why" over and over until the answerer reaches, often unsuspectingly, the root cause.

Example of the Five Whys applied in business:

1. *Why did that machine suddenly stop?* Because it blew a fuse.

2. *Why did a fuse blow?* Because the fuse wasn't the right size.

3. *Why was the wrong size in the fuse box?* Because one of the engineers put it there.

4. *Why did the engineer do that?* Because somebody in the supply room issued the wrong size fuse.

5. *Why?* Because the stock bin for fuses was mislabeled.

Example of the Five Whys applied at home:

1. *Why did you come home late?* Because I ran out of gas.

2. *Why did you run out of gas?* Because I had no money.

3. *Why did you have no money?* Because I went to the mall.

4. *Why did you go to the mall?* Because I needed another pair of shoes.

5. *Why did you need another pair?* Because I lost my other pair.

Go and See for Yourself
(Genchi Genbutsu)

To know the problem, you have to see the problem. Hearsay has no place when striving to be the best.

Once a problem or root cause is identified, decision makers must go to the source and see it firsthand for themselves so it can be quickly and effectively solved. Otherwise, they run the risk of misdiagnosis or inattention that can inflict further damage down the line. Since quality has long been a separation point from competitors for Toyota, the culture does not react well to ongoing product flaws, which erode brand power if not fixed quickly.

One of the most revered principles at Toyota is *genchi genbutsu,* which means going to the source. It involves providing a swift response to small problems that may have large consequences if allowed to continue without remedy, as well as to problems that are large and costly from the start. Going and seeing is required by employees of all levels at Toyota, from entry-level workers to senior-level executives.

In manufacturing, *genchi genbutsu* typically means a visit to the production line. Through the years, Gary Convis has made many such trips himself, taking a short walk from his second-floor office overlooking the assembly line to see a problem firsthand. Get him talking about the go-and-see principle, and the examples come in bunches. When asked to name one, he mentions a buzz he heard during postproduction quality checks coming from underneath the front interior panels of a sedan made at the plant.

When told of the vehicle panel–buzzing problem, Convis walked to the assembly line, stopping at the assembly station suspected to be the source of the trouble. For 15 minutes or more he worked underneath a partially assembled vehicle on the line before determining that a small screw was not being completely tightened in the process, allowing a washer to rattle and cause the buzz. The screw was one of six being tightened in the dark. Because assembling team members could not see the screw, they did not know it was not being fully clamped. In response to the finding, Convis personally shut down the entire assembly line for half an hour, costing the company hundreds of thousands of dollars in productivity but sending the message that quality comes first, no matter what. Also, his personal visit to the assembly line to get underneath that car and look for the problem showed the power of solving through seeing firsthand.

This technique is used in other aspects of Toyota's business as well, particularly those related to emerging technologies and trends. It dates back to founder Kiichiro Toyoda's trips to the United States in the mid-twentieth century to learn, by going and seeing, how Ford was building vehicles more efficiently than other global automotive manufacturers. Today, Toyota still takes a "go to the source" approach when considering new applications or initiatives for the future. That is how Toyota learned first about hybrid technology before patenting the process internally, and that is how it determined after years of study how it would build its new full-size truck, the Tundra. By owning the design, conducting a thorough investigation, and implementing in-house, Toyota reduces competitive and marketplace risk.

"We want to have control," says Convis. "If it is a core issue, we will start as infants, benchmark, go and see and learn, then we will try our own hands at it. This may take us a few generations, but as we do it and improve, we control our own destiny."

6

||||||||||||||||||||

Raise the Bar to Unreachable Heights

[Toyota] somehow said, "We're going to be the best." And that's how they build cars like the Camry.

—Dick Landgraff, former Ford vice president
in charge of the 1996 Ford Taurus program

CONSUMERS ALWAYS LIKE PLEASANT SURPRISES. Giving the customer more than they expect is the best advertising a company can do. While their competitors spend money *telling* customers how great their products are, risking the backlash of broken promises, Toyota wins them over one at a time by actually *giving* them more.

Toyota makes its customers smile long after they drive their newly bought vehicles off the dealer lot, giving them more tangible value than they would have gotten from any other company for a similar product at the same price. Toyota goes beyond the old business adage "underpromise, overdeliver." The carmaker has earned thousands of customers over the years by raising the standards for its vehicles so high that some of them have sold well even without direct and explicit product advertising. When a product is way above the competition in quality and value, says Jim Press, "we don't have to tell people; they see it." One of the best examples of how Toyota strives to overdeliver may be the creation of its luxury division, Lexus—widely recognized as one of the world's premier brands.

Throughout the 1980s Toyota engineers and designers in Japan had been working on a project intended to set an entirely new standard for luxury vehicles. Tired of Toyota being typecast as a manufacturer of small, affordable, efficient vehicles, Yukiyasu Togo, Toyota's chief U.S. sales executive at the time, had advised the company to build a car that his executive friends—drivers of Mercedes-Benzes, Audis, BMWs, Jaguars, and Volvos—would purchase. (The Toyota Corolla, while a fine car in the compact class, was hardly one-size-fits-all.)

The new luxury car would blend sleekness and sophistication with functionality and reliability to create a value proposition for the wealthy. It would be an expensive car that lived up to its asking price by far surpassing the quality of competitive products. Their original idea was to create the full-size LS400 sedan—roomy, powerful, and easy to drive—and launch it as the ultimate vehicle in the Toyota lineup.

Then-chairman Eiji Toyoda spearheaded the Lexus initiative. In 1983, he challenged team members with a simple question: "Can we create a luxury vehicle to challenge the world's best?" Code-named F1, the project was about giving Toyota's growing legion of customers something to graduate into when the company's more functional, conservative cars no longer met their needs. In Japan, Honda was three years away from launching its Acura brand, and Nissan was in the planning stages of launching the luxury line that would become Infiniti. Toyota's aim was to build the single best vehicle money could buy. Company executives were not planning a new brand, nor were they interested in merely developing a flashy new product. The objective was clear: Build the best luxury vehicle in the world.

Under the direction of chief engineer Ichiro Suzuki, who carefully studied competitors in the luxury class like the Mercedes 190E, the BMW 528e, and the Audi 5000, Toyota launched a program to build a one-of-a-kind car. Unlike Ford, which in later years purchased Volvo and Jaguar for billions of dollars to add luxury to its lineup, Toyota sought to create a signature product lineup organically, from within. This approach would give Toyota complete ownership while allowing it to set standards so high that consumers would have no choice but to take notice: Once they test drove the new, impressive car, they would abandon other older favorites in favor of Toyota's new creation.

"The car is not something that sits around," said Suzuki. "It's something that needs to move around. So I thought, I want to build a car that beats Mercedes-Benz in the most basic function a car has, its driving performance."

Toyota's research team visited the United States in the spring of 1985 to live a life of luxury and learn the tastes and preferences of American luxury-car buyers. After living in a rented home in Laguna Beach, California, for several months, the team reached many conclusions, unanimously deciding that luxury-market vehicles had many weaknesses. A Mercedes-Benz, for instance, had a cramped interior and conservative styling. The Audi had a poor reputation for quality, and BMW, while stylish and sporty, sold so many cars that their product became more common than elite. By bringing together the best ever in quality, styling, and service, Toyota would meet and exceed the original challenge laid down by Eiji Toyoda.

Little, if any, expense was spared. Over the course of five years, Toyota invested $1 billion and employed some 60 designers, 24 engineering teams, 1,400 engineers, 2,300 technicians, and 220 support workers to develop over 450 prototypes. Out of this, a production model of the LS400 emerged in 1989. A striking vehicle with an identity all its own, the LS400 shared no noticeable characteristics with other Toyota products. Its roomy interior, sleek panel, powerful V8 engine, and all-wheel drive left all luxury competitors in the dust. Its impressive debut took place amid flashing cameras and smiling Toyota executives at the 1989 North American International Auto Show in Detroit.

Toyota had made the big investment, betting heavily on its future to substantially raise the bar, and won—developing a one-of-its-kind product that reset all standards. But in response to vociferous encouragement from Robert B. McCurry, one of Toyota's earliest and most respected American employees, the company would up the ante even more.

McCurry was a World War II veteran who had excelled as a two-way star in football at Michigan State in the late 1940s. He was a flashy but effective front man in sales for Chrysler long before Lee Iacocca flashed on the scene. Joining Chrysler as a district sales manager in 1950 and becoming the general sales manager by 1960, McCurry was known for pioneering the automotive rebate with his famous "Buy a Car, Get a Check" Dodge promotion featuring Joe Garagiola in advertisements that ran during the halftime of Super Bowl IX in 1975.

With a big personality that matched his football-player physique, McCurry understood the importance in business of providing customers and allies with the proper care and support. When he retired from Chrysler in 1978 to a quiet life in Southern California, he told friends and family he was done with the automotive business for good. However, when Toyota offered him the chance in 1982 to manage the Los Angeles sales region, he couldn't turn down the close-to-home opportunity. As the company expanded in the United States, so did McCurry's role and influence, both domestically and with executives in Japan, including members of the Toyoda family.

As one of just a few key American Toyota employees at the time, McCurry had a way of working with the Japanese, much like Jim Press does today. He approached them humbly but did not shy away from voicing strong opinions when he felt it was important. Over the years, McCurry would campaign for many radical changes he believed would help in Toyota's American market. For instance, McCurry was instrumental in shaping Toyota's North American dealer base into a highly loyal and interactive partnership. McCurry convinced Toyota's executives to treat their American dealers exceptionally well, thereby inspiring heavy stock orders and motivated sales efforts. He pushed for Toyota's first full-size American truck, getting one in 1993, and for a smaller number of dealers provided with more support, getting that as well.

In 1986 Toyota became the first nondomestic automaker to sell more than 100,000 units in a single year. With plans underway to build its first American assembly plant and stakes on commitment to the U.S. market rising considerably, the company relied heavily on McCurry's marketplace expertise. McCurry argued that Toyota's original plan to simply add the

LS400 to its existing vehicle lineup would confuse buyers, minimize the company's opportunity, and shortchange the phenomenal vehicle's potential. He told Togo that the luxury vehicle needed its very own brand, with unique dealers and service, to fully meet all its potential. Togo agreed, and made the case to Toyota's executive committee. McCurry's victory in convincing Toyota to establish a separate brand for its luxury vehicles would prove critical for the company in its trek to the top of the global automotive business.

The Lexus brand was launched in the United States in late 1989 with two models. Within two years, Toyota's new brand was the largest car import in sales, with more than 70,000 units sold. Today, Lexus is the largest luxury brand in the United States, with more than 300,000 vehicles sold each year, and the fourth largest in the world in sales volume. It receives more awards for quality and customer satisfaction from J.D. Power and Associates than any other automotive brand in the world. In 2007 Lexus was named to *Business Week*'s top ten list of "customer service elite" brands, along with the Four Seasons Hotel, Cadillac, and Starbucks. Lexus's quick ascent is quite remarkable.

By contrast, Ford purchased the luxury brand Jaguar in 1989 and has done everything but kill it since. Several years

---

How Lexus beat better-established competitors like BMW, Mercedes-Benz, and Jaguar:

1. Unprecedented quiet ride while maintaining stability and control
2. Elegant interior and exterior styling with highly functional controls
3. Powerful, smooth-running engine yielding better gas mileage

ago, for instance, the company tried to make the niche brand a mass-market product, building Jaguars on Ford platforms. Consumers rejected it, of course, and Ford has been working ever since to rebuild Jaguar's reputation.

For Ford in 1989, buying Jaguar was a big investment in the future, with hundreds of millions of dollars risked so the company could have a luxury brand, but it was barely raising the bar. Jaguar vehicles appealed to luxury buyers with their unique styling, but the British brand was also known for its mediocre quality and subpar service. Ford's decision to forgo developing unique luxury products in-house in favor of purchasing and attempting to integrate another company with a drastically different operating culture resulted in more confusion than synergy. Over time, the Jaguar would prove to be a perennial money loser that detracted from Ford's overall corporate brand.

While the Lexus story highlights Toyota's ability to set its sights exceptionally high and then clear the bar, it did not happen without its share of problems and obstacles. It was indeed a learning experience for a company that prides itself on its ability to learn and adapt. Its commitment to building the world's best vehicle was costly. Budgets were blown away as engineers and designers spared no cost in reaching the objectives. Toyota's executives realized that better planning would be needed in the future for such costly product development. Poor cross-communication in the Lexus's development led to a lot of unnecessary waste.

Shortly after the Lexus launch, Toyota was adapting again, continuously improving by streamlining its development processes to eliminate costly duplication and needless work and expense.

"It was the first time the DNA which had created such great

products for Japan created one for America," says Jim Press, who worked closely with Robert McCurry for many years, adopting his passion and support of dealers, and his active role in product and brand development.

Redefine Classes with Standard-Setting Products (or Service)

When buyers get more for less, they are typically happy. Many industry observers say Toyota gives customers an average of $2,500 more in value per vehicle compared to competitive vehicles from the same class. That is why a Nissan executive, when told in 2003 about cost cuts announced by Toyota, said the company's products were "so overengineered" that millions in cost reductions would still not diminish their vehicle quality enough to bring them down to their competitors' levels. That is also why Toyota for years has been rocketing to the top while General Motors, Ford, and Chrysler have watched their domestic market fall dramatically.

By building and positioning products to be leaders in their class, Toyota maintains an effective value relationship with its customers. It's an unspoken promise that keeps most customers coming back again and again. Somewhere along the way, most Toyota owners realize that the vehicle they bought is worth more than the ones they could have bought; the resale value is frequently higher, and the service bills are usually lower. Rather than feeling buyer's remorse, they report ongoing satisfaction that contributes to Toyota's growing brand strength. Give customers more than they expect, and they'll keep coming back for more, time and time again.

In the history of Toyota's evolution from a middle-of-the-pack enterprise into a global leader, the restyled 1992 Camry sedan stands out as an excellent example of how the Japanese automaker builds customer loyalty. It's a textbook case of how setting high quality and value goals for specific products or services can improve the image and strength of the overall company and build a loyal customer base. Through a restyling effort in the early 1990s that improved the vehicle well beyond the competition, Toyota made the Camry into America's perennial best-selling car.

In the early days of Toyota's business in the United States, the automaker did well with reliable, effectively priced models like the Corolla, a compact car. Known for their low maintenance, high gas mileage, and affordability, Toyota's cars were widely seen as sensible and functional. The brand implied value and conscientiousness. When domestic automakers saw consumers make a noticeable shift to the smaller, better-gas-mileage cars during the oil shocks of 1973 and 1980, they began searching for their own product answers to Toyota's Corolla and Honda's Accord.

Ford came up with the Taurus, a midsize sedan hailed as America's response to foreign car competition. With curved, futuristic styling that elicited nicknames like "jellybean" and "flying potato," and an aura of red, white, and blue, the car became the best-selling vehicle in America immediately upon its 1985 launch. It saved Ford, which was teetering on the brink of complete failure in the early 1980s.

Desperate for a savior, Ford's then-CEO Philip Caldwell told Ford product planners to come up with a radically different car. The Taurus did not exactly raise the bar in terms of engineering and quality, but its individuality proved effective. In 1992 it unseated the Accord as America's best-selling car when

Ford moved more than 400,000 units. Considered by many industry analysts at the time as proof that American domestics could not only compete, but, more importantly, win, the Taurus became Ford's "see what we can do" rallying cry.

Exceed Expectations in Every Way

A competitor far in the lead is difficult enough to catch, much less pass and leave in the dust. However, just as the football team that takes the lead in the second quarter doesn't always win the game, the Ford Taurus eventually lost ground to Toyota's powerful, multidimensional response.

The first generation Camry, built in Japan, debuted in the United States in the early 1980s. The car quickly gained popularity as a front-wheel drive compact sedan and as a hatchback. A solid, no-frills vehicle, it relied mostly on the same qualities that made Toyota's other products popular—affordability, efficiency, and low maintenance. When Toyota opened its Georgetown, Kentucky, plant in 1988, the second-generation Camry made its debut. The hatchback was replaced with a wagon, and the domestically built car developed an unusually loyal consumer base in the United States. Ford's Taurus was still the marketplace leader in sedans, though, and the Camry had the disadvantage of being primarily a Japanese design that was built and sold in America. Recognizing that the Camry was good, but not good enough to be the market leader, Toyota began to work on a project that would dramatically change the fortunes of global auto manufacturing.

The year was 1989, and Robert B. McCurry, along with Jim Press, was dissatisfied with the new, third-generation Camry that was to be introduced in the early 1990s as the answer to

Ford's Taurus. It was still a Japanese design at heart, and while it would prove effective at marketplace maintenance, it would not allow Toyota to meet its full potential by capitalizing on both quality and design. Like its predecessors, the third-generation Camry was going to be reliable and value-oriented but generally staid and lacking the flair needed for the American market. McCurry and Press lobbied executives and managers at Toyota's headquarters in Japan to take the vehicle back to the drawing board and see if more could be done to put the Camry in a class of its own.

Basing the design on a Lexus platform, which provided more room and an engineering base that had proven exceptionally effective just years before, designers and engineers approached the new Camry much like they had Toyota's luxury brand: No expense was spared. The company had been earning money in the late 1980s, but cash was not exactly gushing from the company's coffers. Still, they got the green light upon urging from the United States sales team to raise the bar so far on the new Camry that the competition would have difficulty responding. The result of the significant added expense was an engineering work of genius that delivered far more value to the customer than comparable vehicles like the Taurus and the Accord.

Not only was the 1992 Camry more powerful, roomier, and sharper in design, but engineers had added hundreds of extras, such as passenger air bags before they were mandatory and an aluminum block engine, which cost $50 more per vehicle, even though it was of no visible use to customers. When Ford engineers studying the Camry tried to figure out why the Camry's designers added the block engine when customers would never know of the added value, all they could come up with was Toyota did it simply to make the car "the best."

When the more sleekly designed, arguably overengineered Camry hit dealer showrooms, customers responded positively and competitors like Ford were shocked—no, stunned. At the time, the over-the-top Camry was arguably the best midsize sedan ever built. The program cost Toyota millions, which, combined with the expense of the Lexus launch, caused the company to begin looking for more effective and less costly ways to develop new products. Still, the value to customers and damage to competitors was already done.

The Taurus held on to number one in sales for several years after the 1992 Camry launch, but this was mostly because Ford continually dropped thousands of units into unprofitable fleet sales just to keep factory lines running and to keep the car artificially on top. The Taurus may have been America's best-selling car, but as many as 60 percent of the units sold were to outfits like Hertz rentals. Insiders at Ford knew they had a problem: If the Taurus was not restyled as the best in class, its future success was questionable. So, in the early 1990s, Ford's executives authorized one of the most ambitious vehicle initiatives in the company's history: the Taurus remake.

Initially, the Taurus redesign was intended to best Honda's Accord, the top-selling car at the time. But when Ford team members checked out Toyota's new Camry during the research phase, they quickly learned that they had a new car to beat. Customers were still favoring the Accord, but the Ford team knew the Camry would soon take over; the vehicle was undeniably a wonder for the price. No other car in the class came close. When Ford engineers took a Camry apart piece by piece for study, many became mesmerized and others panic-stricken by the obvious quality, suggesting it was frightening to think Toyota could make a car so good.

Dick Landgraff is the former Ford vice president who was charged with leading the Taurus restyling program and who wrote the project's mission statement after test-driving the 1992 Camry. Wrote Landgraff: "Deliver a product competitive with the Japanese on Quality and Function and Better in Styling Features and value. Beat Camry."

The statement became almost an obsession for Landgraff and the team, and Ford poured in millions of dollars in support just as Toyota had done for the Camry. The Taurus program was riddled with discontent and indecision, though; the Camry had set the standards so high that they seemed unreachable. Throughout the two-year development process, Landgraff and others found themselves vacillating between respect for and resentment of Toyota's accomplishment: "Did Toyoda—the guy who runs the company's name is Toyoda— did he suddenly have the idea one day?" asked Landgraff in 1995. "Did it bubble up from the bottom? Bubble down from the top? Did it have—you know the Japanese—consensus? It's overblown, it isn't quite as consensus-oriented management as you might think—but did they consense [sic] on this over twenty years? I don't know how they did it. They somehow said, 'We're going to be the best.' And that's how they build cars like the Camry."

Ford's new Taurus was launched in 1996. In 1997 the Camry overtook both it and Honda's Accord to become America's best-selling car, a position it still held in 2007. The Taurus met with harsh reviews, and Ford did very little to update it again, allowing it to die a slow death, sustained only by heavy fleet sales. Finally, in 2006, Ford ceased production of the Taurus, killing one of its best brands. The company did, however, announce in 2007 that it would rename the struggling Ford 500 the Taurus, resurrecting the brand, but the damage from ineffectively chasing the Camry had already been done.

For Toyota, the 1992 Camry and the development of Lexus validated the company's ability not only to duplicate its success in designing and building for the American market, but also to do so raising the bar to greater heights than ever before in the company's history. With its bigger interior, more power, and unequaled engineering for a midsize sedan, the Camry also proved that Toyota could be a leader in more than just small, lower-priced vehicles. By developing a product that slotted a class above the competition but cost the same as some in the class below, Toyota exceeded customer expectations and greatly enhanced its brand. Still the best-selling car in America today, the Camry, in its sixth generation, is built in the United States, Australia, and Japan and is considered a luxury vehicle in some markets despite its midsize class.

Create Value Across the Board

Being the best is about giving more, in all areas. Customers expect companies to make a profit, but unexpected added value is often the difference between good and remarkable products. Not every project can be the development of a line like Lexus or a car like the Camry. Some products will be good, not revolutionary. But the little things, the unseen extras, create marketplace differentiation and separate the winners from the also-rans. Toyota provides extra engineering in vehicles across its product lineup that could be cut for the benefit of cost savings without the customer ever noticing the difference.

Some industry observers argue that is exactly what Nissan did in recent years to fuel its revival. The company took engi-

neering costs out, making interior knobs plastic in some instances, while adding a more creative design and sexy extras
that let them charge the customer more. The result was soaring Nissan profits for several years, allowing the company to
rebound from the near financial disaster it suffered in the late
1990s. But as the excitement about Nissan's new designs died
down, growth flattened and the brand's power, while improved,
was still nowhere near that of Toyota.

With its Sienna minivan, for instance, which competes closely
with Honda's Odyssey, Toyota spends extra dollars to provide a
seamless door. On the Odyssey, a faint line can be seen where
body parts come together. The customer may never notice, but
that extra design quality is always there, a kind of Toyota touch.
Similar examples can be cited across the board. Take the cross-
over small-SUV category, which includes the Ford Edge, the
Nissan Murano, and the Toyota Highlander—three vehicles vy-
ing for the same customer. Ford's Edge, which debuted in 2007,
was talked up by company spokesmen for more than a year as
the type of vehicle that would make Ford competitive into the
future. Most critics agree now that the Edge is an improvement
for Ford, but many suggest it is not too different in styling from
Nissan's Murano, which came out years before. Granted, a list
of standard Edge features provided to customers at no extra
charge make it a compelling buy over the Murano, but one
must also factor in Toyota's Highlander.

While it's not quite as stylish as the Edge or the Murano, the
more conservative-looking Highlander has significant advantages in terms of how much value and engineering and how
many extra options buyers receive for their money. Stability
control, a computerized function that tells a vehicle if it is skid-
ding in a direction different from what the driver wants, comes

standard on the Toyota Highlander—something that many consumers might gladly accept but not fully appreciate.

Stability control does not come standard on the Murano. To get it, consumers must pay $750 for the option, then another $4,400 for another required option to make it work. For the buyer, that's more than $5,000 for one feature.

Toyota does not advertise its vehicles' extra value on billboards, believing it is a battle won over the long haul. Or, as Jim Press says, "We don't have to tell them; they see it. The customer knows." This word-of-mouth customer development works. For proof, just look at how Toyota owns the top two loyalty brands in the automotive industry—Lexus is at the top, barely edging out Toyota.

One reason Toyota can invest more in its products, continually increasing its competitive lead over time, is that it pays far less per car sold in employee health-care benefits. Because the company has neither the number of retirees or the binding benefit contracts that competitors such as General Motors, Ford, and Chrysler have, it earns close to $2,500 more per vehicle sold. If Toyota were running a footrace against the competitors, it would effectively be getting a 50-yard head start. By reinvesting that advantage into giving the customer more rather than just cashing it out, Toyota increases its lead with each passing year.

General Motors, on the other hand, has agreed to one labor contract after another over the years. In addition to paying lifetime benefits to former employees, the company is also bound to pay some employees whose jobs were eliminated through productivity increases. So, while the company operated as the world's largest automaker for many years, it was far from the most effective, putting vehicles onto dealer lots handicapped by nearly $2,500 in employee benefit costs while Toyota vehicles were strapped with barely more than $200 of the same. Said General Motor's Tom Kowaleski in a 2006 interview on PBS-TV: "That's a lot that competitors can use to either reduce the price of the car by that much, [or] put added content without raising the price; put that kind of money, multiplied by several million cars a year, into research and development, new facilities, other kinds of dealerships, dealership development growth, market growth—that's a significant burden we carry."

The fact that Toyota reinvests heavily in products outside of research and development, actually giving the customer more, dispels the common theme that the company is too conservative to spend. Toyota, in fact, spends liberally when study and fact-checking shows the need and long-term benefit. Consider that until 2005 Toyota operated out of a headquarters building in Toyota City that was, to put it mildly, small and dated. It was just four stories tall, with few windows and a nondescript brown façade. The building was as close to a true global headquarters as anyone could find at Toyota, yet it was undoubtedly the most unimpressive main building used by any of the largest companies in the world.

The headquarters building was so decrepit and outdated, in fact, that wind is said to have blown through the window frames when the weather kicked up. The air conditioning was not sufficient in the summer and heating was not sufficient in the winter. Still, Toyota's top executives maintained offices in the building until a more suitable headquarters facility was christened in 2005. The new building, certainly, is far more becoming of a corporation with Toyota's global strength and breadth. As one of three buildings that function as headquarters, the

Toyota City structure was built to last well into the future, with quality materials shaping out an airy, roomy, and contemporary design. In comparison to the old building, it serves as a testament to the principle that when Toyota goes in new directions, the company usually spares no expense in doing it right.

7

||||||||||||||||||

Favor Long-Term Strategies
Over Short-Term Fixes

Great results cannot be achieved at once; and we must be satisfied to advance in life as we walk, step by step.

—Samuel Smiles, author, *Self-Help*

UCK RARELY LENDS a helping hand in business. Companies that reach the top put the odds in their favor with
careful long-term planning and execution. Short-term goals
and objectives serve as stepping-stones along the way in a well-
mapped broad plan. Managers and employees who pursue the
quick gratification of large short-term rewards such as quarterly profits or large bonus checks while eschewing the long-
range plans of the organization are serving themselves first
while hindering their companies' chances for greatness.

A short-term focus seems to make sense for individuals
whose bonuses are tied to increased stock prices and quarterly
and annual profits. Cashing in on a fad or the latest trend may

set a company up for long-term problems, but sometimes that's what it takes to keep the company stock afloat. Once the trend runs its course, executives can bail out with a nice bonus and hand the company's leadership, problems and all, to the next person. Unfortunately, this is precisely what has happened to hundreds of U.S. corporations over the last decade, in which CEO turnover has reached unprecedented levels.

In the global automotive business, this scenario is precisely why many Western companies have recently seen a revolving door of top-level executives. One after another, they have implemented divisional strategies designed to impact short-term results. Sure, Ford, General Motors, and others have discussed and even implemented aspects of long-term plans, but their execution has more often been decidedly shortsighted.

For instance, multiple experts advised GM that its continued unprecedented incentives, intended to drive volume so the company could meet short-term sales goals, were damaging its brand and teaching consumers to expect hefty discounts. Similarly, Ford was warned for years that flooding heavily discounted products into unprofitable fleet sales just to maintain lofty sales rankings would seriously harm the company's future. On paper, it looked good for Ford to be able to proudly call the Taurus number one. But in reality, it was a foolish ploy, eroding the long-term value of one of its best and most branded products. In implementing such tactics, today is given precedence over tomorrow.

Toyota could have joined the game, plowing its products unnecessarily into the marketplace for short-term benefits. The company chose instead to proceed step by step. Today, the Camry is number one and the original Taurus no longer exists.

"We would not [push products into unprofitable fleet sales]," says Jim Press. "If we did, it means we did not build the car the customer wants. [Extreme product discounting] undermines the value and is not really fair to the customer. Should not everybody pay the same price?"

Favoring long-term strategies over the quick fix is a well-established practice for Japanese businesses. In addition to this cultural tendency, Toyota focuses on the future largely because its leadership feels that respecting its people requires a long-term outlook. Thus, the company makes plans in intervals of 3, 5, 10, 15, and 20 years and makes decisions on everything from product development to marketing in those time frames. If an initiative is not good for the future, why do it today? For example, Toyota could have easily shifted from a pull system to a push system of production several years ago, leaping past global competitors in size. Instead, the company opted to stick with its longer-term strategy, which has yielded profitability and consistent growth since 1951.

Says Gary Convis: "Our foundation is stability. Our stability comes from a long-term approach."

Make Daily Decisions That Benefit Long-Term Plans

Toyota sacrificed quick (and potentially short-lived) success in favor of an overriding long-term strategy because, says Press, "it is the right thing for our customers." Over time, the company has nicked away at the wildly fluctuating results of its competitors and has eventually gained a decided advantage of sustained success over cyclical mediocrity.

During the mid-1990s, Toyota's earnings were hardly impressive. It earned an average annual net income of about $2.5

billion from 1993–1998, compared to $4.5 billion for GM and $7.3 billion for Ford during the same period. Needless to say, employees of both General Motors and Ford were living well; executives received millions of dollars in bonuses.

The obvious reason the automakers thrived during that period was the onset of the SUV boom, a consumer phenomenon created and fed jointly by General Motors and Ford. Beginning with the Explorer and continuing through the mammoth-sized Excursion and Hummer, American automakers designed, manufactured, and heavily promoted the largest and most profitable vehicles ever made. Consumers responded enthusiastically, helping profits to soar at both GM and Ford.

In making larger and larger vehicles, U.S. carmakers didn't figure into the equation the fact that SUVs get the lowest gas mileage of all vehicles and that the gasoline crises caused by the oil shock two decades before nearly sent several American automotive manufacturers into bankruptcy. Nor did they take into account that fossil fuels are limited and that gasoline, although readily affordable and available in the mid-1990s, would one day again grow scarce. Worst of all, they did not understand the long-term ramifications of their decisions. Shareholders and employees would ultimately suffer, and the management of those companies would find themselves searching for new ways to revitalize and reinvent their firms.

Toyota could have easily joined the others and chased the SUV trend of the 1990s, changing its long-term focus to reap short-term gains. The company already had natural positioning and an understanding of the market; in 1957 it had built and sold the first Land Cruiser, the precursor to the SUV. Yet even though Toyota participated in the SUV segment throughout the boom with vehicles like the 4Runner and Sequoia, its commitment was moderate and proportionate and consistent with its overall product strategy. Put simply, it did not bet its future on a trend.

A close look at more than 15 years of comparative numbers from Toyota, General Motors, and Ford quickly tells the story and demonstrates why long-term strategy usually trumps short-term tactics. Not once since 1951 has Toyota lost money in a full reporting period, providing growing strength through sustainability—one of the truest tests of a great company. At General Motors and Ford, the numbers reveal net income losses with periodic growth spurts.

One cannot help but wonder how Ford earned $21 billion in 1998 only to lose $12 billion less than a decade later, or how General Motors lost more than $10 billion twice in just 15 years. Nor can one help but ask how Ford in early 2007 posted the worst quarter in its 103-year history while Toyota posted its best quarter ever (earning more than $3.6 billion in net profit). The answers to these questions, of course, are the same: short-term strategies that were eventually exposed as shortsighted due to changing trends and economic conditions.

In essence, Toyota remained a car company while larger competitors allowed themselves to become shaped by the image of trucks. One Corolla yielded far less profit than one Chevrolet Suburban, but building gargantuan vehicles was not in Toyota's immediate plans. Toyota executives, therefore, did not abandon their long-term strategy to chase the next new thing before it burst; they moved methodically, and executed the plans that had been in place for years.

As General Motors, Ford, and Chrysler were investing significant resources in building bigger and bigger gas-guzzling vehicles, Toyota in 1993 initiated in Japan a costly and highly secretive project named Global 21. The twenty-first century was less than a decade away, and former Toyota chairman Eiji Toyoda believed the company needed to put its time and money into creating a unique product for the next generation of customers, shareholders, and employees.

Some of the Global 21 project objectives:

1. Develop a small sedan with unprecedented fuel efficiency for a mainstream consumer vehicle.
2. Make the car environmentally friendly.
3. Create more interior space than previously offered in compact cars.
4. Maintain consumer affordability so the vehicle is not merely a corporate talking point.

Run by Risuke Kubochi, Toyota's general manager of general engineering who was previously in charge of the Celica program, the initiative was a major undertaking at a time when Toyota had nowhere near the sales or resources of its larger competitors. Toyota engineers had previously been working to develop hybrid engine technology, a system that reduces gasoline usage by integrating electric power, and Kubochi and the high-level executive committee he reported to ultimately agreed it was the best match for Global 21.

After several years in development, the project resulted in the revolutionary Prius sedan. Using Toyota's own hybrid technology, dubbed the Hybrid Synergy Drive, and patented design, the Prius was the world's first bona fide twenty-first-century vehicle intended for sale on a mass, commercial level. Its development was one of the most difficult challenges in the history of global product design, engineering, and manufacturing. Total costs, including the development of the hybrid technology, exceeded $1 billion. Difficulties arose all along the way, but the project received strong encouragement and direction from the highest corporate levels.

"There will be great significance in launching the car early," said former Toyota president Hiroshi Okuda, who took charge of the company in the midst of the Prius project. "This car may change the course of Toyota's future and even that of the auto industry."

After the Prius team worked literally around the clock to meet Mr. Okuda's targeted 1997 public release date, the car was launched in Japan to media raves—it received the country's "Car of the Year" award—and higher-than-anticipated consumer demand. Two more years passed before Toyota offered the Prius for sale in the United States. Some critics said introducing the model to such a large market was a mistake, since Toyota was still subsidizing the vehicle's price tag to make it affordable compared to other compact cars. In truth, the move was costly to Toyota in short-term dollars, considering that the company was increasing the number of vehicles it sold at a transaction loss. Also, some of Toyota's American employees were not immediately convinced a small, hybrid-engine car was needed as the prosperous 1990s ushered in a growing demand for bigger and bigger vehicles.

Like most of Toyota's top North America executives, including Jim Press and Gary Convis, Don Esmond began his automotive career as an employee for Ford. He worked 11 years for the Dearborn, Michigan–based company and also spent time in the United States military. Personable and plainspoken,

Toyota's director of sales in North America recalls wondering out loud how much sense the Prius addition made to the company's product line.

"[Toyota's Japanese leadership] brings this vehicle to me and says, 'We want you to sell this,'" Esmond says. "'Customers will want this.' I had been with the company at that time for almost 20 years and I understood what we are about. As the sales guy, I'm scratching my head. But I drove [the Prius] and realized the performance is good . . . this is a real car. We got strongly behind it."

In 2007 Toyota was expected to sell 430,000 units of the Prius and other hybrid-engine power vehicles—a 40 percent increase over 2006 levels. Sales of the Prius did slow a bit for the company—mostly, executives said, because the public assumed there was a waiting list for the cars. But overall sales of the fuel-efficient car continued to soar, even as gasoline prices in the United States leveled off. In addition, Jim Press said hybrids are now profitable since volume has increased and engineering and manufacturing are more efficient. Toyota now offers hybrid engines in such popular products as the Camry sedan. Its competitors are also getting into the act, releasing hybrid cars of their own. However, Toyota is widely considered the leader in alternative transportation and maintains a position of strength.

While competitors like Nissan, another Japanese-based company, grapple with the merits of hybrid technology (Dominique Thormann, Nissan's senior vice president for administration and finance in North America, argued in late 2006 that "hybrids today are not a very viable economic proposition; it's still a loss-making proposition."), Toyota continues with its

Toyota's vehicles available with hybrid engines in 2007:

- Prius
- Highlander
- Camry
- Lexus GS 450h
- Lexus RX400h
- Lexus 600h L

The Toyota Sienna minivan is scheduled to have a hybrid engine optionally available by 2010, and Toyota aims for every product in its lineup of cars, trucks, and SUVs to have a hybrid engine option by 2030.

commitment, winning thousands of new customers from Japan to the United States with each passing month.

"In the beginning [American] customers were mostly people some would define as tree huggers because nobody was thinking or talking much about gas and the environment," Esmond says. "Fast-forward to today and it is clear that hybrid technology has moved solidly into the mainstream. This was not a PR stunt by the company but a long-term view of the world and needs."

Don't Overinvest in the Flavor of the Day

Peter Drucker, the great management writer, warned managers of the danger of short-term thinking for decades. In his 1964 book *Managing for Results,* he explained that "any leadership is transitory and likely to be short-lived." He also warned of "unnecessary specialties," and "the specialty that needn't be one." U.S. carmakers fell into several of the traps Drucker described. They specialized unnecessarily, operating under the assumption that more of the same would yield positive results.

Take General Motors as an example. The automaker was making near-record profits in 1999 on the strength of its SUV sales at just about the time Toyota introduced the Prius to the U.S. market. Considerably more profitable for GM than sedan sales, products like the Tahoe and the Suburban had the widest margins in the company's history. The bigger the vehicle, the bigger the profits, GM executives reasoned. So why not just create the biggest one of all?

Just as Toyota poured almost $1 billion into the Prius development, General Motors signed an agreement with a company named AM General to jointly produce a consumer version of a military truck, the Humvee. An acronym for High Mobility Multipurpose Wheeled Vehicle, the Humvee had served the U.S. Army, Marine Corps, Air Force, and Navy well since the early 1980s. Prominently featured in Operation Desert Storm in 1991, the Humvee was highly praised by the military for its combination of strength and flexibility. A family car, however, it was not.

GM did not see it that way, though. AM General had launched a civilian version of the Humvee in 1992 that it called the Hummer. Known as "the world's most serious 4×4," the truck provided consumers the ultimate in rugged mobility. It was like an SUV on steroids—big and bulky but handy to have around in case a war broke out. By 1999, GM and AM General reached a joint agreement giving GM the exclusive rights to the Hummer name. By investing millions to develop the new Hummer H1—an upscale, more commercialized version of the civilian original—and create an entire large-scale automotive brand, GM was attempting to capitalize on the profitable SUV craze in a huge way. Never mind that the H1 traveled just 10 miles or less on a gallon of gas and the price after luxury add-ons was more than $100,000. Remarked automotive analyst Eric Merkle: "It's really one of those over-the-top vehicles. It doesn't really have much of a place in everyday society. You can't put it in the parking ramps. Parking spaces can't accommodate it."

General Motors reportedly poured almost as much money into the Hummer brand as Toyota did into the Prius and hybrid project, all seemingly because SUVs were trendy at the time. By 2006, with gas prices soaring amid international turmoil and many consumers waking up to the sad gas-guzzling reality of their SUVs, the Hummer brand was already getting a makeover. The H1 was dropped altogether in favor of a smaller Hummer lineup.

Toyota, on the other hand, today owns almost all of its hybrid technology and is widely considered within the automotive industry to be well positioned as the twenty-first-century leader in alternative technology and products. The company's sales, net income, and stock price have soared while its one-time larger competitors have struggled mightily, blaming their woes on a difficult marketplace.

Is Toyota just lucky? Hardly, according to Jim Press. "Based on all of the factors in consideration at the time . . . with talk of global warming and the limit of fossil fuel," says Press, "[Toyota's leaders] asked themselves back in the early 1990s, if you were going to build a new franchise today, what would you invest your money in to better serve customers in the future?

Both [GM and Toyota] had the same opportunities. You make choices, you live with them. For Toyota, the short term is not what we are after."

Don't Watch the Stock Price

As in any improvement initiative, changing the focus of decision making from short-term to long-term is often not successful without a commitment to implementation. Working for the long term is a mind-set, requiring a clear understanding that what is good for tomorrow is best for today. Prioritizing goals is key, as is understanding that the leading objective is something other than besting the previous month's sales record.

The focus should be not on positive numbers themselves, but on the things that contribute to them, like better serving the customer and contributing to society. Positive numbers may be a cause for celebration and a confirmation of a job well done, but they cannot be used as guides or to influence core principles. For Toyota, such an approach has allowed the company to look beyond the short-term pressures of quarterly reports. Says Jim Press, "Our goal isn't to sell more cars. Our goal is to give our customers more quality. If we do a good job, our sales will go up . . . but our goal is not higher sales and profits. We work for the customer. We strive to give them peace of mind."

Toyota's commitment to a long-term approach begins at the top. The principle dates back to the company's founding and remains both a practice and conviction today. Press recalls receiving this wisdom firsthand during a dinner at Dr. Shoichiro Toyoda's home in Japan. The company's stock price had experienced a run-up earlier in the day; investors had apparently liked some Toyota-related news report or rumor. Making dinner conversation with Dr. Toyoda, Press mentioned that he saw the closing stock price, assuming Dr. Toyoda was thrilled as one of the company's larger shareholders.

His dinner partner responded quickly: "I do not watch the stock price. If I did, I might make bad decisions for the company," declared Dr. Toyoda definitively.

8

||||||||||||||||||

Learn the Customer,
Live the Customer

We make things everybody thinks we should make.

—Katsuaki Watanabe, president, Toyota Motor Corporation

HUBRIS IS THE SILENT KILLER of businesses. More than overspending, more than poor execution, and more than expensive labor contracts or pension plan obligations, excessive arrogance has probably tripped up more managers and corporations than almost any other boardroom blunder. Toyota has long recognized the adverse influence arrogance can have on effective decision making. The company is quick to admit that it doesn't always have all the answers.

Says Toyota's Jim Press, "We know we don't know."

Had managers at the Big Three U.S. automakers echoed similar sentiments over the years, there is a good chance that they could have avoided many of the problems that have haunted them in the last decade. Of course, they didn't, and Toyota has bypassed all three in nearly every measure, from customer service to quality to profitability and, ultimately, to sales.

Avoid Hubris

In 1983, General Motors was in the midst of a massive reorganization. A domestic surge in sales by foreign upstarts like Honda, Nissan, and Toyota had hurt the American automaker. That year, GM debuted four of its new cars on the cover of *Fortune* magazine, claiming it had designed the cars in teams, emulating the Japanese automakers' design style. GM pitched the cars as the embodiment of innovation. This *was* the future, GM executives claimed. At the time, GM still controlled almost 45 percent of the United States market—a figure that seems almost inconceivable today—and was expected to earn several billion dollars that year. The company's success made believers out of everyone.

GM executives claimed that the company's newest sedans featured on that *Fortune* cover would be so successful that they would leave their competitors in the dust for years to come. Despite GM's over-the-top promises, those four cars—the Chevrolet Celebrity, Pontiac 6000, Oldsmobile Cutlass Ciera, and Buick Century—were exactly the same size, the same color, and relatively undistinguishable from one another. The vehicles also had whiny transmissions, subpar quality, and no features to distinguish them from much of what General Motors had been selling for decades. Oddly, too, the Buick Century cost more than the Chevrolet Celebrity, even though both products were made by the same corporation and were, as one automotive authority said, "virtually identical." Those cars did define the GM's future, but not in the ways the company intended.

Despite all of the boasts, GM's 1983 lineup was both a disappointment and a symbol of everything that was wrong with the company. GM had a bad case of hubris and there were no signs that they were going to get rid of it anytime soon.

Ford and GM have remained at the top of the industry when measured by sales volume, but maintaining their lofty positions has cost them in other key areas. Even when sales have been strong, profits at Ford and GM have fluctuated wildly, depending on the strength of the economy. The dizzying ups and downs of their fortunes may lead one to believe that the success of the entire automobile industry is dependent upon the economy. History shows otherwise, however, revealing how arrogance and indifference toward the customer can derail any company, regardless of its size or competitive position.

Recall the attitude of former Ford executive Dick Landgraff, charged with heading the 1996 Taurus program. The company spared no expense in chasing after the Camry and as a result was forced to price the car well above initial projections. When asked during a meeting with reporters about the high price tag, Landgraff apparently became annoyed.

"I'm not concerned about affordability," Landgraff reportedly said. "If Joe Blow can't afford a new car, tough (expletive deleted). Let him go buy a used car."

Such a mind-set is a far cry from Samuel Smiles's promotion of business through humility, or W. Edwards Deming's customer-focused management principles. Ford eventually had to tackle the pricing problem and ultimately offered a "bare bones" version of the Taurus at a greatly reduced sticker price, but the damage was already done.

Today's car buyers are more confused than ever, thanks to too many similar products spread out over too many brands.

One of the root causes was overzealous executives who acquired smaller competitors rather than build from within. Ford, for instance, has eight brands under its umbrella after acquiring brands like Jaguar, Land Rover, and Volvo. General Motors has seven, including Hummer and Saab. Toyota, the world leader, has just three, and each was built internally and is clearly defined with easily distinguishable products.

Also, an examination of Toyota's vehicle lineup reveals one important fact: The leading products that the company sells today, like the Corolla and Camry, are the same products the company has been selling for years. Engineering and design improvements have upgraded these models to meet evolving needs and tastes, but Toyota rarely drops unwanted vehicles on consumers. The company typically avoids this by developing products with direct customer research and input. Ask Toyota executives how the company has so many marketplace hits and you'll usually get the same typical response: "We're a company that listens to the market," says Jim Lentz, executive vice president of Toyota Motor Sales USA.

However, no company is immune to hubris. Toyota has certainly fallen prey to it on occasion, making similar missteps to its U.S. counterparts. Among the more notable product flops in the company's history are three vehicles developed in 1999 as part of a program known as Project Genesis. Under the direction of Yoshimi Inaba, then-president of Toyota Motor Sales USA, the project was intended to attract more youthful buyers. This market segment fell outside of Toyota's core market. The Corolla, for example, was massively popular for years running, but its mainstream styling did not always suit young buyers looking for more edgy, niche products.

A Toyota study group led by Inaba aimed to introduce new

products that could be sold as a "marquee within a marquee" through Toyota's United States dealer network, resulting in the Celica, the MR-2 Spyder, and the Echo. These vehicles were advertised independently of Toyota's traditional lineup but were sold on dealer lots alongside the other models. Project Genesis represented a departure from the Toyota way, in that its lineup was brought to market more on the basis of Toyota's internal beliefs than marketplace research. The initiative was driven from the top rather than the customer level. The MR-2 was an underpowered two-seater with no storage room, and the Echo and Celica did not connect with young buyers emotionally. All three products were canceled within five years, providing a chapter in Toyota's history that resembled similar botched launches by American and other carmakers. The lesson was not lost on Toyota's leadership: Making new products without adequate customer input is a recipe for failure.

However, because the concept of serving young, trend-conscious customers with unique products still held appeal for Toyota, the company retooled Project Genesis into an independent brand, Scion. The brand was launched in 2003 as a separate marquee, and the company recognized that significantly more market research was needed to better understand young buyers the way it understood its mainstream and luxury customers.

Take to the Streets and Observe

Jim Press was a driving force behind Scion's creation. He noted that a couple of small but quite distinctive Toyota car models were selling well in Japan and wanted to try exporting those to the United States under a new brand. The idea was not to set up an entirely new dealership (like Lexus), but to give Scion an individual identity under the Toyota system, creating a culture within a culture.

Aimed at young Generation Y consumers, the first Scion vehicles were sold by young, hip salespeople. When they were readily accepted by the marketplace, Press pushed hard for original product development specifically for the United States. He gets credit for the Scion tC, the brand's sporty coupe and first model to be developed specifically for the U.S. market. Once the Scion development engineers got the message, they closely studied America's Generation Y consumers, employing Toyota's philosophy of *genchi genbutsu*, going to the source to see and learn firsthand. To serve the customer, you have to know the customer, intimately. So, just as Toyota had sent the Lexus designers to live and learn a hyperluxurious life, the company employed a grassroots fact-finding mission to find out what young buyers would want in the Scion.

Instead of simply building vehicles executives and designers guessed young buyers would want, Scion team members went to parks and neighborhoods in Southern California to observe and hang out with young skateboarders and other edgier denizens. They learned that their intended audience didn't want anything that would be seen as mainstream, commercial, or something older generations would drive. The resulting vehicle designs were so outrageous that no executive at GM or Ford would have ever approved them, one industry manager remarked. The first Scion looked like little more than a small box; another closely resembled a large egg. Toyota sold just more than 10,000 Scion units in 2003, a figure small enough to make many large companies give up on a new concept. But inside Toyota there was near-universal consensus, says Jim Press, that since the customer was served, the customer would respond.

Sales built slowly, with little marketing, as the company let buyers discover the Scion on their own and build word-of-mouth buzz. By 2006, the approach was clearly working: Toyota sold more than 175,000 Scions for the year, most to buyers between the ages of twenty and twenty-five. The company also had unprecedented success in capturing the attention of Generation Y consumers through highly targeted, anti-brand-style marketing. Such campaigns included events on California sidewalks with DJs and music, skateboards and T-shirts.

Some of the younger participants did not know that the goal of the event was to sell cars, but Toyota sees each one as an opportunity to build customers for the future while capturing critical market information.

"We want to capture customers who would not have considered the Toyota brand," says Scion corporate manager Steve Haag. "We don't want to necessarily sell them Scions. We want them to get to know our brand and hopefully consider something in the Toyota family because they like who we are."

This approach fits in with Toyota's long-term strategy of winning and earning customers rather than grabbing market share by forcing products on them. Just as the company manufactures with a pull system rather than a push system, it carefully cultivates customers by giving them products that reflect their desires, needs, and wants. Of course, Toyota does not always get it just right; immediate successes like the original Lexus or the 1992 Camry are rare. But by continually listening and learning, being willing to adapt, and maintaining a long-term view, Toyota is able to translate customer feedback into improved products with long marketplace life cycles.

"From my perspective, we have never had the goal to be

number one for sales," says Don Esmond, Toyota Motor Sales USA senior vice president. "We have had the goal to be number one with the consumer. We try not to get hung up on how great others say we are; we just try to remain focused on the customer. When the smoke clears, if we maybe end up on top, that's fine."

Perhaps Toyota has been driven by necessity to be more customer-sensitive through the years. When the company first arrived in the United States, some buyers soundly rejected its products because it was obvious they were not designed with Americans in mind. Toyota's first minivan, as a case in point, sold moderately well in Japan but was a total bust in the United States, because, as Esmond recalls, it was not user-friendly. The van was launched just before Chrysler's first minivan reached market and attempted to define a new segment for soccer moms and families. It had no walk-through capability, and users had to lift the driver's seat just to change the oil. The van clearly did not meet the needs of American consumers.

Recognizing the vehicle's shortcomings, Toyota adjusted and evolved, taking steps to become a true American company by listening to customers and its American sales team. Designers added front-wheel drive, reconfigured the oil change issue, added walk-through capability, and found a winner with a vehicle renamed the Previa. The van sold well in both the United States and Japan. But while the Previa managed to gain popularity in the United States, it still had flaws that detracted from the customer's experience, such as a big hump between the first and second row of seats where the engine was located. So Toyota kept tweaking its minivan design, eventually developing the Sienna, which became one of the more popular minivans.

Meeting different customer needs outside Japan has been Toyota's strength, but American automakers have not always done as well in satisfying their non-American customers. GM and Ford spokesmen call their companies global, and the companies' annual reports deliver the same message. With operations from Europe to Asia, they do have significant global presence, but they generally adopt a take-it-or-leave-it approach to their foreign customers, mostly shipping out vehicles designed and produced in the United States for American consumers. European tastes and American tastes are not the same, however. What sells well in Evanston may not sell well in Edinburgh and the other way around. Toyota's Scion began as a Japanese product, but it was revamped for an American audience before it sold effectively in the United States.

The Nissan Versa is a compact car that the company designed for and sells in Europe and Japan, but changes were made to personalize the product for America. "Whenever you do a global product you just have to remember there are details that have to fit (each specific market)," says Press.

Simply put, winning means listening to and responding to the customer, not just telling them what they need or should want. Toyota has been able to sell the Previa in the United States even though its original design was intended for Japanese customers, but only because the company was and is willing to listen, learn, and humbly make compromises to find middle ground.

Says Jim Press:

- Learn the customer
- Live the customer
- Empathize with the customer

Don't Fight Changing Trends

Many Toyota employees and executives readily admit that "putting the customer first" is an old corporate cliché. The difference between Toyota and other companies that talk about serving the customer, however, is that Toyota's entire structure is actually based on doing it.

But doing it is easier said than done, though, making it one of the company's greatest challenges. After all, what worked well one day may not work so well the next. Trying to force marketplace repetition despite shifting tastes and trends because that is what factories are programmed for is a costly, losing battle.

For years, automotive insiders and industry observers have claimed that to be a major failing of America's Big Three automakers and the primary reason Toyota has been stealing thousands of customers with each passing month for years in succession. As one hourly-wage employee for Ford told me, his company tends to build cars and then find the parts from around the factory to make them work. Likewise, he said, designers and engineers tend to consider what plants are already configured for, creating from there. And why not? The strategy worked for years, keeping the company among the biggest in the world (as long as nobody counted the internally forced fleet sales). Toyota, on the other hand, he said, has a reputation for building its vehicles for the customer, not for the plants or the parts.

The fact that what worked one moment will not always work the next can be hard to accept. The stubborn gambler returns time and time again to the same slot machine that once gave a large payout, hoping to get another; the automaker that made billions selling oversized vehicles continues to pour money into even bigger vehicles while largely ignoring other aspects of its business. GM and Ford consistently bet the company's future on lineups laden with oversize trucks and SUVs, which paid off handsomely for more than a decade. When all the signs pointed in different directions beginning in about 2001, Ford and GM ignored them. Thus, no matter how detailed Ford's restructuring plan was under former CEO Bill Ford and no matter how many cost cuts General Motors made, the harsh reality by the end of 2006 was that American automakers were out of touch with customers. They were trying to shove more profitable products at buyers because it was largely all they had to offer. On the other hand, Toyota recorded sales of 450,000 Camrys and almost 400,000 Corollas to garner 15 percent of the American market.

"All the old rules of the game are gone," said James P. Womack, cofounder of the Lean Enterprise Institute. "We're now in the reinvention phase." The 2006 chart listing sales data for the 15 best-selling cars and trucks in the United States read like premature obituaries for a couple of formerly dominant products. Ford saw an 18.1 percent decline in sales from 2005 for its F-Series pickup, which had been America's best-selling truck for almost 30 years, and, as mentioned earlier, ceased production on its flagship Taurus sedan.

In 2007, the irony of these industry changes was evident to all as Toyota finally entered the full-size pickup truck business with the launch of its new Tundra. The company had soundly beaten its once-larger competitors by exceling in the car business while the other automakers focused almost solely on large trucks and SUVs; then, just as GM and Ford began to focus on cars again, Toyota entered the full-size pickup market.

For years the three-quarter-size Tundra pickup had been sneered at by fans of hardcore open-bed products like Ford's F-150 and Chevrolet's Silverado. Competitors openly suggested that Toyota was not even a legitimate player in the full-size truck business, since big trucks are seen as the quintessential American vehicle and Toyota's almost-big truck seemed like a wimpy foreign imitation.

But when Toyota decided to enter the full-size pickup truck market, building a new manufacturing facility in San Antonio, Texas, the company one-upped GM and Ford by spending time in the field learning about potential customers. Rather than stick to the stereotypical male truck-driving audience, however, Toyota's engineers immersed themselves in the South, the heart of America's truck country, hanging out at NASCAR events, staying overnight at ranches, and tagging along with families traveling in RVs. They found that in Texas and other states where big trucks are popular, women drive a significant number of pickups, as do many older consumers not willing to give up the power and payload. Toyota uncovered many of the little aspects of the product that would make a difference to these consumers.

For example, since not everybody driving a pickup truck resembles a stereotypical truck driver, the Tundra's tailgate is outfitted with gas-powered lifts, so closing it is possible with just two fingers. No more lift and slam, hoping for a latch.

Designed almost entirely in the United States, the truck is bigger and more powerful than both the Silverado and the F-150. While this move seems counterintuitive when one considers how Toyota has beaten GM, Ford, and Chrysler in recent years with smaller, more efficient vehicles, Toyota executives claim the full-size truck is just part of their effort to offer a full lineup to its customers. The company aims to sell just 200,000 Tundras a year, relying on across-the-board product strength from the Prius, Corolla, and Camry. The company's entry into the full-size truck market, according to Press, was not based so much on following trends as it was on meeting the demands of customers for a larger, more powerful vehicle. Also, the foothold in that market gives Toyota yet another profitable position from which to grow the company.

Ford executive Mark Fields called the full-size Tundra just another example of Toyota trying to be "very American." Press counters that it's more about Toyota trying to *serve* American customers.

Never Stop Chasing the Moving Target

When asked in 2007 how Toyota was handling proclamations that the company had reached number one status globally as both an automaker and corporation, Tomoni Imai, a 25-year Toyota employee and group manager of the corporate communications department, was quick to laugh. "Mr. Watanabe," he says, "will never say Toyota is number one." The reason, Imai explains, is that rankings of size, profit, and customer satisfaction reflect what the company did yesterday. Being number one isn't possible because Toyota is focused primarily on the customer, and the customer is always changing. "The customer," he says, "is a moving target. The customer always wants more."

While working in sales for Toyota's European operations shortly after joining the company, Imai visited a dealer with some engineers to gather input related to a new vehicle in development. For many years, the dealer had also represented an American automaker in Europe, but not once, he said, had that company asked him for information or insight into the customer.

Imai was pleased to see research garnered from that visit incorporated into the new car's design. When the vehicle was launched successfully, the engineers were already back in the field, seeking ways to improve the next generation. Imai began to understand the need for continuous improvement with a focus on the customer. Going and seeing what the customer wants provides Toyota with the ability to meet more of his or her needs and demands, he says, but the customer will always want more from their vehicles, making the quest for customer satisfaction a mission that has no end.

9

‖‖‖‖‖‖‖‖‖‖‖‖‖‖‖‖‖‖

Take Time to Study,
Then Implement with Speed

When the decision is made to act, we move fast in execution
because everyone is already fully bought in and in accord.

—Jim Press, former president, Toyota Motor North America

MAKING DECISIONS is not nearly as important as making
the right decisions.

At Toyota, the pressure to meet surging global product demand with factories around the world running at near capacity
is as intense as at any global corporation. Its meet-customer-
needs philosophy requires that it make cars as fast as customers
want them. But that does not mean the company will make
hasty decisions or charge ill-prepared into new frontiers simply
to beat out competitors. On the contrary, Toyota makes its decisions more on the basis of collected facts than individual opinions, and facts take time to gather and properly assess.

In keeping with the company's culture of humility, the

general belief at Toyota is that brashness and moving forward ill-informed leads to problems and poor decision making. By carefully vetting all possibilities and all influencing factors, Toyota's decision makers ensure that they don't proceed with half-baked ideas. This style of operating has given Toyota a widespread reputation as a conservative company, a firm that moves slowly. However, insiders tell a much different story. While Toyota takes all the time it needs to gather facts and reach consensus, it moves more quickly than competitors once decisions are made.

Move Forward Step by Step

Few events in Toyota's history illustrate the company's careful planning better than its arrival on the United States manufacturing scene in the early 1980s. The company had been selling cars in the United States since 1957, when it first imported the Land Cruiser and Toyopet. Toyota's initial entry into the American market was tepid at best, but by 1964, when it introduced the compact Corona—its first vehicle designed specifically for the American market—the company was recognized for its well-built, unusually reliable cars. Costing less than $2,000, the Corona was more affordable than comparable American products and known for running with little service until the body literally rusted apart.

Toyota introduced the popular compact Corolla to the American market in 1967, and by 1971 it was selling more than 300,000 Japanese-made vehicles in the United States. Such sales numbers prompted executives at American automakers to take notice of the Japanese company, but no one considered Toyota a serious threat. GM, Ford, and Chrysler treated Toyota like it was an annoying fly that merely needed swatting. Jim Press recalls laughing when his former boss Henry Ford II suggested that Ford was going to push the Japanese "back into the ocean" with a revolutionary new car that would undermine both Toyota's quality and its value, winning back all the customers the foreign company had taken.

"A car called the Pinto," says Press.

But as the Corolla became America's most popular small car and Toyota's commitment to continuous improvement, quality, efficiency, and affordability yielded a full lineup of American products, the company became a formidable niche player in the market previously dominated by the Big Three automakers. In 1975, Toyota passed Volkswagen to become the leading U.S. import. Toyota's commitment to the relentless pursuit of improvement made the once-small Japanese company a fierce global competitor, and many American industry watchers began to speculate that the Toyota Way might one day overtake the ways of the Big Three.

Opportunity abounded for Toyota, particularly in the United States, and pressures mounted on the company to build cars where it sold cars—in America. The natural move for Toyota would have been to jump at the opportunity, moving as Nissan did—headstrong into United States manufacturing. But Toyota's distinct advantage was its strict adherence to its long-standing manufacturing and general business philosophies. Could *kaizen* translate to foreign soil and to employees unfamiliar with the virtues of the emerging Toyota business principles? Toyota's top executives were not so sure.

They knew that American automakers struggled with quality, and it was hard to tell if corporate mismanagement or the workforce itself was to blame. So, as important as building cars on American soil might have been to the immediate financial future, Toyota decided to test the waters before plunging into United States manufacturing.

Gather Facts Firsthand

While there is nothing in the Toyota rulebook that precludes hiring outside consultants, its leaders believe that nothing can beat the benefits of hands-on learning. Closely tied to Toyota's "go and see for yourself" principle, the company has long practiced a methodical fact-gathering process that typically begins in the field with qualified reports and recommendations of experienced employees.

The company could have easily hired an automotive industry consultant to help them begin manufacturing cars in North America, but instead, Toyota pursued the previously unimaginable—a partnership with General Motors to build cars in the United States.

Ford and Chrysler vehemently opposed the New United Motor Manufacturing, Inc. (NUMMI) joint venture, which Toyota and General Motors formed in 1984. The other companies feared GM would gain so much advantage by learning manufacturing from Toyota that its powerful position as the world's largest automaker would be strengthened beyond measure. Without exceptional manufacturing techniques and efficiency, GM was formidable; with Toyota's manufacturing know-how, GM might become unbeatable.

NUMMI went forward despite an investigation by the Federal Trade Commission and a lawsuit by Chrysler and Ford. The FTC approved the venture, seeing it as "a potential role model for U.S. companies" that would provide "a wider range of automobile choices for consumers." Toyota invested $100 million, and GM provided a shuttered plant in Fremont, California, for the joint venture. According to the agreement, Toyota would play the leading role in manufacturing, sending Japanese managers to teach the Toyota Production System. Five thousand former GM Fremont employees were offered jobs. In an unprecedented move, the United Auto Workers agreed to work under NUMMI labor terms, allowing its members to learn the TPS system without union interference in return for employment at the facility.

The NUMMI/UAW labor agreement, based on "mutual trust and respect," included several unusual terms for a typical American contract, including:

- Nonconfrontational problem-resolution procedures based on discussion and consensus.
- Advance consultation with the union on relevant business issues.
- Minimally defined job classifications that provide work flexibility.
- A "no strike" provision over production or safety standards.

Toyota's aim was to see if TPS could successfully be implemented in America and to learn more about the customs, difficulties, and opportunities of manufacturing in the United States. Therefore, the company, under the leadership of then-chairman Eiji Toyoda and then-president Shoichiro Toyoda, sent many of its top-level managers and executives to NUMMI; in fact, Tatsuro Toyoda, Shoichiro Toyoda's brother and the nephew of Eiji Toyoda, was sent to the United States to head NUMMI.

General Motors, on the other hand, sent a rather random collection of mostly mid-level managers to NUMMI. GM, one could argue, had the most to gain, since its manufacturing techniques were universally considered inferior to Toyota's; however, 16 mid-level GM managers went to California to learn TPS from some of Toyota's highest-level managers and executives. They joined NUMMI eager to learn the system and manage the hourly employees, but it was not that simple. American managers could not begin teaching NUMMI hourly employees directly until the Japanese managers and executives believed they had wholeheartedly embraced the spirit of lean production. In effect, they were serving an apprenticeship, expected to studiously learn with patience and on-the-job training. According to Steve Bera, one of the original GM managers assigned to NUMMI, "We had to move in progressive fashion until [Toyota's managers] were ensured of the fact that we could give back to the organization, teaching it to the workers. We had to become evangelists [of TPS] and if they did not feel that we could teach it from the heart, we could not move on."

When Steve Bera was asked to join NUMMI, he was initially hesitant, until his wife reminded him how much better the weather is in California than in Detroit. Also, he knew a good opportunity when he saw it. He could see how much bureaucracy was hurting GM and how much TPS could potentially help the company. Besides, he wanted to learn. Bera also knew that the Japanese working at NUMMI were there to learn how to work within American communities, how to motivate American workers, and how to work with American suppliers. The proposition seemed like a win-win situation for him, learning their management techniques while teaching them American culture.

For both NUMMI and Toyota, it was a win-win proposition. The factory began producing the Chevrolet Nova for GM in December 1984, and—for a GM launch—both the reviews and the product quality were unusually impressive. Within 18 months, NUMMI was also producing the Toyota Corolla FX16—the first Toyota to be made on American soil—and the quality was close to Toyota's Japanese standards.

While the Americans wanted to celebrate these early victories, Toyota's lead team members reminded them that good was not good enough—too many defects meant too many unsatisfied customers. "I remember when NUMMI first won a [J.D. Power and Associates plant quality] silver award," says Gary Convis. "We were all patting ourselves on the back like typical American guys. One of Toyota's Japanese managers said, 'Yes, but look at all the defects we had. Yes, we did well, yes, we made money, but now this is what we have to do because we still have these problems.'"

Eventually, the Americans learned the system, and in turn they taught the Japanese employees about Western culture, particularly the social customs both directly and indirectly involved in business. Teamwork took hold, original NUMMI employees say, and the American managers learned much about the Toyota Way of making things. As the plant matured over several years, GM's NUMMI managers were dispersed to different regions and divisions to implement TPS as individuals rather than as a collective team.

"That was the fallacy in the whole deal," says Bera, who left General Motors to become a consultant. "We were sent out there to learn everything we could on the efficiencies of how Toyota built product . . . the quality, decision making, training, purchasing. . . . The best thing GM could have done is take the best practices and put them into a new concept plant, but there was so much resistance. A lot of the old guard would say, 'It will never work in my plant,' and there were so many issues with years of UAW contracts . . . they just let us scatter."

GM proceeded to implement TPS piecemeal. Toyota, on the other hand, moved slowly and collectively, using the experience to determine whether or not the company could manufacture vehicles in the United States with the same standards used in Japan. When the answer provided by the NUMMI experience was a resounding yes, company executives proceeded rapidly with planning and building a dedicated Toyota manufacturing facility in the United States. Had the NUMMI venture not worked so well, Toyota would likely have held off.

"If NUMMI did not work," says Dennis Cuneo, an attorney who helped Toyota set up NUMMI and navigate FTC approval before becoming a Toyota executive, "it could have set [Toyota's North America plans] back for some time."

In other words, NUMMI was an experiment. It resulted in Toyota's first North American manufacturing facility—the Georgetown, Kentucky, plant—established in 1986. In 2007 that plant employed 7,000 team members to build such popular vehicles as the Camry, Avalon, and Solara and is widely recognized as one of the most efficient facilities in the world.

Once Toyota decides to act, the company moves very quickly to the execution stage, having already removed the most obvious barriers during the planning stage. The merits of the first American manufacturing facility were considered, literally, for years, yet once plans were made to build the Georgetown, Kentucky, plant, the facility was up and running within two years. Four years later, in 1990, it won the coveted J.D. Power and Associates Gold Award for initial quality.

Buy-in Builds Speed

One of the key factors fueling Toyota's rise to the top in its industry is its speed in execution. Compared to its rivals, it moves extraordinarily quickly, despite its somewhat misleading conservative image. The company's planning is thorough and methodical, leading to efficient and streamlined execution—one of the critical factors of Toyota's success.

Long known in product development circles for continually improving its vehicles after launch, Toyota has parlayed its quick execution into an ability to provide the latest styling and features to its vehicles in the quickest manner possible. As a result, the company takes vehicles from concept to consumer faster than any other automaker in the world. Toyota's average time to market, from clay freeze to the start of product production, is 24 months. American automakers average 28 to 34 months.

This speed is driven by the Toyota Product Development System, which relies on many of the principles of TPS and Toyota's overall business approach: lean, cross-functional cooperation and collaboration, and cross-company buy-in and support. It is how Toyota got its new Tundra pickup truck to market so quickly once it decided to enter the competitive full-size market. The company had studied a full-size truck option for years, gauging the long-term viability of the truck market and the company's best way to enter it. Once the decision was made, however, Toyota opened a new plant in San Antonio, Texas, and the product development team took a clay freeze model of the truck to production in just 24 months.

Compare that with Ford's product development process some years earlier for its best-selling F-150 pickup. Ford engineers and designers began working on a new truck model in

1999, but cost overruns and delays pushed development back a full year, forcing a late-2003 launch. While sales of the truck soared, the extra six to eight months in development caused budget overruns and gave competitors time to get their products to market and close the competitive gap.

Similarly, in the mid-1990s General Motors experienced a dreadful production start-up at its Lordstown, Ohio, plant for its subcompact Chevrolet Cavalier and Pontiac Sunfire. Supply shipments were in disarray, but nobody worried too much, since—as Rick Wagoner, the current GM CEO and former president of its North American operations, said—it was tough to make a "net, net, net profit on small cars anyway."

As with all automakers and manufacturers, Toyota experiences launch delays as well. The company's Tundra pickup was delayed almost two months. Also, a new Corolla planned for a 2007 North American launch was delayed until 2008 because of quality concerns.

Overall, however, Toyota routinely moves much quicker than its competitors, due to both its deep and thorough planning and its streamlined, bureaucracy-free implementation. The result is a product development timeline that frequently bests competitors by as much as 30 percent. That is critical time in today's automotive marketplace, where stale products typically move slowly on showroom floors. This speed advantage, along with its consistently high quality standards, is allowing the automaker to increase the already considerable gap that exists between Toyota and its competitors.

It is also why Toyota was able to take on Ford and GM as aggressively as it did. Toyota's leadership knew that its product development time had become a genuine and significant competitive advantage. In 2000, Toyota remarkably topped 7 of 16 total categories in the J.D. Power and Associates study for initial quality, while no competitor placed first in more than two categories.

"We don't move slowly," says Jim Press, "if you consider the actions other companies take. We move quickly to market, but we spend three-quarters of the time planning and considering so implementation occurs rapidly."

Toyota's engineering, design, and sales teams work together to move forward on the basis of shared, fact-based, and information-supported platforms. They keep company precepts like focusing on the customer, eliminating waste, and continuously improving at the forefront. The approach takes out costly delays caused by individual or group hypotheses and keeps all the parts fitting together during the design and building phase. Essentially, the left hand and right hand work on the same pieces at the same time without distraction or resistance, getting the job done more quickly and efficiently.

How to move faster with thorough decision making:

- Take a holistic approach employing cross-functional teamwork.
- Keep the customer at the forefront of decisions.
- Progress simultaneously from fact-based platforms.

10

||||||||||||||||||||||||||||

Let Failure Be Your Teacher

It is a mistake to suppose that men succeed through success; they much oftener succeed through failures. Precept, study, advice, and example could never have taught them so well as failure has done.

—Samuel Smiles, author, *Self-Help*

TOYOTA'S CULTURE READILY ACCEPTS that the greatest companies are also flawed companies that routinely make mistakes. As long as people figure into the equation, there will always be errors, both in the millions of minute tasks as well as in the weighty, large-scale decisions that affect the company's future. At Toyota, imperfections are not overlooked or avoided, but treated with reverence and attention and openly acknowledged as highly important.

At Toyota, flaws are highlighted with visual and verbal signals, like the line-stopping andon cords, pulled the moment manufacturing problems are detected, and other such alarms. Once a problem is identified, team members work together to fully flesh out and fix the mistake so quality can be quickly restored. To avoid finger-pointing and emphasize problem solving, team members make an effort to reach the root cause through such strategies as the Five Whys.

"You don't blame [employees]," says Gary Convis. "Maybe the process was not set up well, so it was easy to make a mistake."

Toyota is now considered one of the world's greatest companies in customer satisfaction, quality ratings, sustained profitability, and robust growth. During its ascent, Toyota has had the reputation of being invincible, a corporation that rarely missteps, while its competitors have made multiple high-profile mistakes through the years, such as signing labor contracts they can't afford and struggling with unreasonably high product recalls. Unfortunately for them, they seemed to have learned little from their blunders. Toyota has avoided the really major gaffes—debacles like Ford's Pinto and the Explorer/Firestone tire controversy, and General Motors' periodic financial meltdowns over the past two decades. It's not that Toyota doesn't make mistakes—far from it. The difference, though, is how Toyota typically responds to the mere hint of a problem.

Parlay Mistakes into Success

Among Toyota's most significant opportunities to learn from one of its mistakes occurred in the United States in the early 1990s, just before the successful third-generation Camry was launched. The second-generation Camry, launched in 1989 as Toyota's first American-manufactured vehicle, was found by the Center for Auto Safety (CAS) in the United States to have a major safety defect.

Following consumer complaints, the center determined that

some of the cars experienced an electrical malfunction that disabled the power windows and locks. There were several reported cases of drivers and passengers trapped inside their cars for an hour or more. The problem was apparently a failure in the electronic control unit that caused the contacts to "weld" and prevented the doors from being unlocked, even by hand.

A CAS employee reportedly told Toyota officials about the problem. When nothing apparently was done in response, he took the story to *Consumer Reports*, which ran a detailed exposé of the problem. The CAS also issued a press release suggesting Camry drivers carry a hammer in their cars just in case they found themselves submerged in water or trapped in a burning vehicle and needed to break out a window to escape.

In response to the negative publicity, Toyota recalled more than 500,000 of the 1989 Camrys in question. By the time the third-generation Camry was launched in 1992, the vehicle's quality and engineering were so high the episode was hardly remembered, and Toyota's reputation in the United States was never better.

The problem was taken seriously inside the company, though, and the prevailing issue was much larger than the failing windows and door locks. For Toyota to be a trusted brand anywhere in the world, especially in America, its response to complaints had to be far more effective. Failing parts were one thing; inadequate reaction was another.

The leading culprit was found to be poor communication between engineers in Japan (responsible for the car's composition), manufacturing managers in the United States (responsible for the car's construction), and sales executives in the United States (responsible for the car's marketing). Toyota's U.S. presence in the early 1990s was small compared to today, and it was the first time the company had been faced with a quality issue of such magnitude. Also, while Toyota had effectively established manufacturing in the United States, it had not effectively established an effective communication protocol for dealing with such situations. At the time, all of the engineering still took place in Japan, and methods for dealing with problems that occurred outside of Japanese factories had yet to be worked out.

After suffering public embarrassment over the company's slow response to the power door-lock issue, Toyota's leadership in Japan quickly learned that for Toyota to be an effective global enterprise, cross-company communication lines must be opened and feedback from the field must be given the highest priority. New procedures were put in place encouraging managers and executives to "pull the cord" whenever they identified a problem. The result was that Toyota took a giant step toward becoming a more complete American enterprise, with better communication and greater empowerment from its Japanese home base.

Says Jim Press, "You don't learn from success; mistakes are what shape us. We treasure mistakes."

Often in manufacturing the root causes of mistakes lie not with the product maker but with parts suppliers that pass along faulty components to the manufacturer. When Toyota neared the 1997 launch of its fourth-generation Camry, for instance, the on-sale date was pushed back 60 days because of internal quality issues. The company's American sales team was eagerly anticipating the new car, which they'd been promoting to dealers and consumers for almost a year, but they encouraged the delay so the vehicle would be as close to perfect as possible. Just 10 days before the ultimate launch, one supplier uncovered a problem with the car's side mirrors. The faulty mirrors rendered 2,000 already-built Camrys defective and put the twice-delayed launch into further question.

Toyota's North American sales team was engaging in extensive daily dialogue with Alec M. Warren, the manager of Toyota's Georgetown plant, where the Camry was being built. Pressure was mounting for a timely delivery, since dealers were waiting for the new cars to fulfill considerable and growing customer demand. But since an emphasis on cross-functional dialogue was one of the key outcomes of the earlier Camry recall incident, everyone clearly understood that addressing a bad situation aggressively and openly was better than the embarrassing alternative. The decision was made to hold the vehicle launch until the defective mirrors could be repaired. Warren told employees about the problem, and 400 volunteers came down to work 24 hours a day until all of the mirrors were exchanged with new ones, getting the Camry to the marketplace as quickly as possible.

Make Problems Top Priority

Managers and employees tend to report good news first, usually because that's what their peers and superiors want to hear. Toyota, policy, however, is to report the *problems* first. When imperfections are completely disclosed, the problem-solving capabilities of the full team can then be applied to remedy the situation. Withholding problems for even a moment is viewed at Toyota as getting in the way of the ultimate quest of continuous improvement.

To get better every day, problems must come first—always.

This lesson is one James Wiseman, Toyota's vice president of corporate affairs for Toyota Engineering and Manufacturing (TEMA) North America, learned early in his career. Ever since, he has adhered to the philosophy that good news can wait until the not-so-good news is thoroughly discussed and debated by fellow employees.

A Kentucky native, Wiseman held several jobs after graduating from Vanderbilt University with an English degree in 1974, including one as a small daily newspaper sportswriter and one as a high school English teacher and assistant football coach. As a businessman in the 1980s, while working jobs as a factory manager for a swimsuit maker and a steel-tubing manufacturer, he became a member of the Kentucky Chamber of Commerce and was named president of the organization.

At the Chamber of Commerce, he was required to report good news first by putting a positive spin on everything. The same was also the case for Wiseman in his other jobs as a journalist and a teacher. He was expected to solve problems on his own rather than discuss them out in the open. "There was always a lot of looking for the silver bullet," says Wiseman, "looking for the big, dramatic improvement. And I had the attitude that when you achieved something, you achieved it. You enjoyed it."

But shortly after taking a communications job in 1989 with Toyota at its new Georgetown plant, Wiseman learned that the automaker operated differently. Led by Fujio Cho, the former president who serves today as Toyota's chairman, the Georgetown facility was the company's first full-scale entry into American manufacturing and there was little room for missteps. As he had in his previous jobs, Wiseman attended the weekly senior staff meetings, led by Cho, and came prepared with a list of accomplishments to report.

At many companies, of course, such a positive approach is

fine, even preferred. Everyone gathers in a meeting room and one positive report after another is made: This week, we fully planned the office party and it promises to be the best ever; this month, I was able to eliminate overtime expense and our profit margin increased 2 percent; this quarter, we sold more products and everyone should get a bigger bonus.

The positive approach, though, did not work at Georgetown with Cho, who had been a student of the Toyota system and principles for more than 25 years. Cho was well-versed in the principles of Sakichi Toyoda and the writings of Samuel Smiles. He believed in conservatism, humility, and never covering up one's mistakes. He was charged with putting Georgetown's manufacturing plant on par with Toyota's plants in Japan, and he was not interested in frivolous discussions during the weekly staff meetings. Instead, Cho wanted to know about the problems plaguing the facility so the team could turn their attention to making Toyota a better company. He demanded unflinching honestly about trouble spots and listened intently.

"I started out going in there and reporting some of my little successes," says Wiseman. "One Friday, I gave a report of an activity we'd been doing"—planning the announcement of a plant expansion—"and I spoke very positively about it; I bragged a little. After two or three minutes, I sat down.

"And Mr. Cho kind of looked at me. I could see he was puzzled. He said, 'Jim-san. We all know you are a good manager, otherwise we would not have hired you. But please talk to us about your problems so we can all work on them together.'"

Wiseman says he learned that even when successes *were* discussed, Cho taught the senior managers to delve deeper and figure out what more could have been done. He made them continually ask, How can we make it better?

"I have come to understand," says Wiseman, "what they mean when I hear the phrase '*Problems first.*'"

The philosophy is not difficult for employees to follow when the top leaders of the company practice it as well. And at Toyota, nobody lives this principle as effectively as president Katsuaki Watanabe. The company's top operating officer took Toyota into unprecedented territory in 2005. Profits were surging and the company was on track to surpass Ford and General Motors and become the largest automotive manufacturer in the world. Watanabe rose to power after eliminating billions in costs over five years, but in the leadership position, he found himself and the company in a precarious situation even as Toyota was making great gains on its competitors.

Because the company focused so fiercely on cutting costs under Watanabe's orchestrated CCC21 program, some industry observers speculated that its longtime lead in quality over its rivals was in jeopardy. Recalls reached an all-time high in 2005—Watanabe's first year as Toyota president—and production glitches were attributed to engineering and development, the areas strained the most by the stringent cuts. In October 2005 alone, the company set a Japanese record for one-time recalls when 1.27 million vehicles, including Corollas and RAV4 SUVs, were summoned for repair to fix defective headlights.

Combined with the subsequent U.S. recalls of Corollas and Prius hybrids due to defective steering shafts, the company that prides itself on quality had a very big problem. The issue was not that Toyota was no longer building vehicles better than its competitors; it was still recalling fewer vehicles than other companies. However, its cost demands had diminished supplier quality, and the consolidation of parts for use on multiple vehicles (ordered to receive volume discounts) meant that when one part was bad, more vehicles were adversely effected. In 2006, recalls dropped, but quality problems continued to the point that Watanabe was deeply concerned. Profits were at an all-time high, yes, but had Toyota jeopardized its long-earned sterling reputation in the name of price cuts?

Watanabe did not focus on the company's good news. At that point in time, he was thinking only of the company's problems, and nobody could convince him otherwise. Embarrassed by the fact that Toyota's quality had been compromised, he called a press conference, bowing in apology and pronouncing, "Toyota's quality has made us what we are today, so we can't afford to let it slip." Many company CEOs would have stood before an audience and talked only of how great the enterprise was doing, setting records, opening new markets, and overtaking longtime marketplace dominators. But that was not Watanabe's way, nor was it the Toyota way. He stood before the cameras, asked for forgiveness, and put problems first. He pledged to do better and named the former head of the company's European operations to the newly created position of senior managing director in charge of quality. Watanabe thus made quality a primary responsibility of executive Akio Toyoda, the company founder's grandson. Internally and externally, the usually reserved Watanabe spoke bluntly, calling the quality issue a "crisis." Watanabe summed up his thinking on this matter in five words: "Problems must be made visible."

In accordance with the principle of dealing with problems first, Watanabe ordered that no recalls be delayed. The company has taken a proactive stance, informing the customer as soon as quality issues are discovered. "Early detection and resolution is the key," he says, "and I'm telling [Toyota] people not to hesitate to recall. That's very important for customers. Rather than extending the period before a recall, or thinking the problem isn't serious enough, the most important thing is to try to service those cars and correct difficulties early on."

The upshot of Watanabe's vigilance in Toyota's otherwise unprecedented period of prosperity is that competitors may have more to fear in the future than ever. In line with Toyota's ability to learn and continuously improve, the focus on quality issues is resulting in higher quality than the company has ever before experienced. The principles have remained the same, from striving for continuous improvement, to taking time to study, to eliminating waste. But now, more tools have been added, from simplifying initial product design, to having deeper involvement with suppliers. Ultimately, Watanabe says, the company can have a robust future and cause to celebrate, but only when problems have been fully addressed first.

"I believe it is vital that we faithfully hold to our belief that no growth can come without improving quality," he says.

11

||||||||||||||||||||||||

Cultivate Evolution

Something is wrong if workers do not look around each day, find things that are tedious or boring, and then rewrite the procedures. Even last month's manual should be out of date.

—Taiichi Ohno, former Toyota executive vice president

TO GROW EFFECTIVELY, you have to be willing to evolve. Toyota proved that business as usual is rarely good enough. Times change, and so do people. What works in one area or region may not always work so well in another. For these reasons Toyota's precepts of business are passed throughout the company among employees as ideals—principles to live and work by—but not as absolutes. The very nature of the aspiration for continuous improvement requires flexibility and change. As a learning organization, Toyota realizes that just because something was done yesterday one way with positive results does not mean that same way will best serve the needs of tomorrow.

Few examples in Toyota's history illustrate this better than the company's introduction of TPS to the United States through the NUMMI joint venture. When NUMMI began in 1984, Toyota's Japanese structure and top management culture were not altogether different from those of automakers in the United States. Toyota's top executives typically enjoyed private offices, wore suits and ties to their offices, and were driven to work by chauffeurs. Bringing the same approach to America would have been natural, if not expected, particularly in light of the Big Three automakers' well-established hierarchical corporate caste system. General Motors, the world's largest automaker at the time, set the tone in Detroit in 1984. At GM, arrogance ruled. It existed in the company's executive suite and ran through manufacturing plants and social clubs and everywhere the company's elite gathered or had authority. The result was "obscene executive privileges and insularity" and management "not wanting to recognize that the world was changing."

The American automotive market began to change in the late 1970s when American consumers started to favor imported Japanese-manufactured cars and Toyotas in particular. The trend continued into the 1980s, bolstered by the oil shock that shifted even more consumer attention to the more efficient foreign-made cars. Detroit autoworkers and executives generally assumed that Toyota's cars sold well in the United States simply because they were less expensive and smaller. Considerable skepticism existed on the manufacturing/quality side of the business, evidenced by such prevalent American claims as "We taught them how to do it."

This sentiment reflected the fact that the first Toyota, the 1930s model AA, was based on a Chevrolet, and the fact that Toyota executives spent time in the 1950s studying factories at Ford. Toyota executives and engineers soaked up everything they could about lean production before quickly improving upon Ford's system. Consumers were buying Japanese cars in greater numbers than ever before, and American carmakers were beginning to wear their resentment toward the Japanese auto executives on their sleeves.

Thus, if Toyota had arrived at NUMMI in 1984 with anything short of the deepest humility, it could have been costly. The company was charged with teaching TPS to GM executives and employees, and the belief at Toyota was strong that its executives and managers must make changes to be most effective in America.

Toyota's concept from the first day of NUMMI operation in California was for company employees to be teachers instead of preachers. Toyota's leadership wanted the Americans to see TPS for what it is—a lean process for greatly improved manufacturing. They did not want to give American workers the impression that they saw themselves as individually or collectively superior. Rather, they wanted the Toyota system to be the center of attention. Therefore, the top Toyota managers and executives at NUMMI abandoned their suits and ties in favor of the established standard company uniform. They also rejected special parking places for higher-ranking officials, instead making the plant parking lot first-come, first-served, and desks were lined up in large rooms so that all employees were positioned as workplace equals.

Never mind that Tatsuro Toyoda, one generation removed from the company founder, was on the job as a lead NUMMI executive. Toyota's original precepts of "be practical and avoid frivolity" and "strive to create a warm and homelike atmosphere" were fully in play from the first day of the company's manufacturing presence in America. The aim was to avoid elitism and autocratic leadership, offering hands-on teaching in something of a democratic environment. Or, as one NUMMI participant said, when Toyota goes into a new environment, "it is almost like starting a church"; the structure is built, people come together, and teachings begin under common, unified principles. The company may have worked one way in Japan, with a more traditional worker-management hierarchy that was typical in America, but Toyota executives were willing to change, operating on the strong belief that new ways of working were needed to take the focus off individuals and draw more attention to the system.

By removing physical barriers like special parking places and plush management offices, Toyota's NUMMI leaders made people and processes the main focus of the joint venture. Meanwhile, global competitors like General Motors and Ford continued to conduct business as usual, holding to the same operational practices that had served them for more than half a century. The labor-management relationship at the Big Three's United States plants is an excellent example of this. The system initially established to benefit workers in the early twentieth century had essentially created a wall between labor and the corporation. This problem was largely overlooked and continued into the twentieth century for the unionized autoworkers.

Adaptation has been key for Toyota in the United States. Following the changes implemented specifically for NUMMI, the company has taken further steps over the years, like abandoning male-dominated business pastimes like golf—"We don't do golf anymore," says Jim Press—and other out-of-office activities that have the potential to alienate some employees. American plant workers never really took to morning calisthenics, for instance, and Toyota dropped that practice in the United States while continuing it in Japan.

Toyota's ability to adapt to the many communities in which it operates, both in the United States and in other markets abroad, may be one of the more important aspects of the Toyota Way. Many who study the company fail to notice this, since the general assumption is that Toyota is a company deeply rooted in traditions. The reality, though, is that Toyota not only adapts to but actively cultivates corporate evolution when change is needed for future improvement. So, while General Motors, Ford, and Chrysler have continued a traditional system of manufacturing in the United States in which management is kept far away from workers both in communication and physical distance, Toyota has morphed, developing a unique system for America that empowers employees and downplays management's power.

"That is a good example of how Toyota can look at a market and adapt to it," says Dennis Cuneo. "They looked at it and saw what needed to be done. That's the beauty of the Toyota system, treating people with respect and whatever it means in a given culture."

View Change As an Opportunity to Learn

The best classroom teachers are learners as well. Toyota's culture is about not assuming one is right but striving to get principles uniformly in place so that rightness ultimately prevails. Therefore, when Toyota sent many of its top manufacturing executives and managers to the United States in the early 1980s to teach TPS to American managers and workers, a primary assignment and expectation was that they, too, would learn at every opportunity, listening, taking advice, and keenly observing the General Motors employees.

The Japanese workplace is traditionally much different from the gregarious American one, in which a coworker is likely to share personal details and invade one's space. In Japan, talking about oneself on the job is viewed as shameful, and workplace social functions are often stiff and formal. American managers tried to help Toyota's NUMMI employees bridge the social gap, and some involved in the process say the Japanese citizens were willing to learn.

"I remember going to dinner at one of the directors' homes early on," says Steve Bera, one of the original American NUMMI managers. "His wife could not sit at the table with the men. My wife would have thrown somebody out over that. This was a custom in Japan."

Another time, Bera recalls, one employee hosted a dinner party in Fremont, inviting eight Japanese couples and eight American couples. Immediately, the Japanese men all went to one table for conversation, leaving the women to themselves. Bera recalls that his wife stepped in, joining the male guests. During a pool game after dinner, his wife jumped in with the Japanese men. They were not offended, Bera says, but they were caught somewhat off guard. Soon, the Toyota employees began to socialize more according to American customs, adapting to the differences.

"They realized," says Bera, "that you can be smart and successful and operational and insert some of the softer side socially as well. You take a look 20 years later . . . the dress, the behavior . . . and Toyota is a very American company."

By paying close attention to the changing landscape and issues America faced as it moved toward and into the twenty-first century, Toyota emerged as a company more in touch with realities and challenges facing both America and the world at large. Following the unfortunate events of September 11, 2001, turmoil in the Middle East, environmental concerns, and the realization that fossil fuels would not last forever nor be cheap forever, more consumers than ever are turning to companies like Toyota, which not only articulate but also act on their vision for the future.

Tennessee congressman Zach Wamp, a Republican member of the U.S. House of Representatives' renewable energy caucus, is widely known as an outspoken leader on the need for assuaging America's dependence on foreign oil and addressing environmental concerns. In 2006 Representative Wamp met with former Toyota executive Dennis Cuneo and chairman and CEO of Toyota Motor Sales USA Yuki Funo, recruiting the automaker for a plant site in his district. Long convinced that Toyota was more in touch with the realities of the new century in regard to transportation, Wamp came away from the meeting an even stronger believer in the Toyota Way. He felt that leaders at Toyota "got it," while domestic competitors remained confused.

"GM and Ford seemed to have had their heads buried in the sand about what was happening in the world." says Wamp. "The [domestic] powers needed to shift gears earlier."

Toyota, on the other hand, forced the issue in America by bringing the first hybrid engine–powered vehicles to market for mass commercial sale. In addition, the first hybrid vehicles were generally well engineered and built, making a strong statement that little if anything had to be sacrificed by consumers wanting to make the leap to a hybrid. The result, says Wamp, is that Ford and GM had "their heads handed to them by Toyota." Consumers responded in record numbers, no longer viewing Toyota as a foreign company with domestic product offerings, but as a very American company.

Need proof?

In 2006, Toyota ranked among the top ten of *Fortune* magazine's "America's Most Admired Companies." The list, which contained no other foreign-based companies, included the likes of General Electric, Starbucks, Dell, and Berkshire Hathaway, and served as proof for Toyota that adaptation in today's global environment is of principal importance.

12

||||||||||||||||||||||||||

Plan Big, Execute Small

The true measurement . . . is not what you have taken, but [what you have] given in return; the same thing goes for a company. We reinvest in America or wherever we are and try to help those who cannot help themselves.

—Jim Press, former president, Toyota Motor North America

THE WORLD'S GREATEST STRUCTURES were built one stone at a time, just as a vehicle is assembled one part at a time. Many components may be small and seemingly insignificant, but each requires individual attention for the complete structure to be properly built. Similarly, by treating the world as a collection of unique but intricately important parts requiring specialized attention, Toyota has grown into a powerful global corporation that resembles a unified collection of smaller, localized businesses.

Just thirty years ago, Toyota was essentially a Japanese company. While it sold products throughout the world, most of its reinvestment in both operations and community occurred in its home country. But as the company expanded its operational footprint, joining General Motors in partnership in California, building more than 10 different manufacturing facilities in America, and adding facilities in Europe, Brazil, China, and beyond, the company lost this centrally Japanese focus. By establishing local and regional presences around the world, Toyota increased its global strength.

This dynamic shift from a centralized entity to a multilateral force with many strong, individualized parts was critical to Toyota's ascent to the top of the global automotive industry and integral to its growing reputation as one of the most effective and respected manufacturing companies in the world. The change is one reason Toyota is no longer seen as a strictly Japanese company.

Interestingly, Toyota leaders agree that this is exactly what has transpired: In America, Toyota has become quite Americanized. But in Europe, Toyota has become very European, while in Brazil, Toyota has become very Brazilian. And the change is even more specific than that. Toyota has also become very Kentucky, due to its presence in the Bluegrass State, and Texan due to its presence in San Antonio. The principle of adapting to serve individuals and communities is rooted in Toyota's respect for people, one of the foundations of its business. The result is a fluid entity of people, processes, and technological systems that serves a multitude of cultures and yields powerful local support for Toyota worldwide.

Toyota's conversion from a Japanese company into a viable global corporation over the past three decades is a bit ironic, considering that it was America's Big Three that first pushed for Japanese automakers like Toyota to build products in the countries where it sold them. Complaining that it was not fair for foreign automakers to build vehicles in other countries where labor and goods were cheaper and ship them into the United States for sale, the Big Three lobbied in the early 1980s for stricter trade laws. Unfair competition, went the argument, made winning in the marketplace more difficult for the most important U.S. companies. The "we taught them how to beat us" attitude was still prevalent among automakers like Ford and General Motors, both of which suggested that Toyota had merely studied their trade secrets and improved upon them in more favorable manufacturing environments. In response, the United States and a handful of European countries imposed limits on the number of imports Japanese companies could bring into their countries and sell.

But even with limits on imports, Toyota carefully deliberated the decision to build cars in the United States. Once the NUMMI experience showed Americans could build high-quality products and Toyota decided to enter the U.S. market with infrastructure (e.g., manufacturing plants), it committed to being more than a Japanese company building products in America; Toyota aimed to become, over time, as American as apple pie, Coca-Cola, or Ford Motor Company.

In Detroit, Michigan, drivers cannot go more than a few miles without seeing Ford's logo across everything from schools to hospitals to downtown buildings. The company's founding family was known for its generosity, and the corporation continued to contribute to its community and America for many years until shrinking profits made large philanthropic gifts far more scarce. A similar story can be told of General Motors. In Flint, Michigan, the birthplace of the American automaker and the home of "Buick City," a 235-acre sprawling manufacturing complex built in 1984 and intended to be an answer to Toyota City in Japan, reminders of General Motors' generosity dangle from one street corner to the next. Yet, in Flint, as in Detroit, these signs are mostly aging. As in Ford's case, such heavy community contributions have become more scarce in recent years.

Toyota, on the other hand, has been moving in an entirely different direction since its arrival in the United States and in other regions of the world. Based on an early principle of Sakichi and Kiichiro Toyoda that placed emphasis on being "contributive to the welfare and development of the country," the company invests substantial time and money resources in the communities surrounding its operational and manufacturing facilities, treating each as a mini–corporate headquarters. Toyota views contributing to Georgetown, Kentucky, as no less important than investing in Toyota City, Japan.

The localization involves more than mere dollars. The Georgetown plant has its own Web site, for instance, that places minimal emphasis on the company's Japanese roots and focuses on the factory and its workers as if it were a single, successful American company. Toyota has invested millions in local public education, and American workers have been given the highest-level jobs at the Georgetown facility. Similar scenarios have played out at factories in Australia, Canada, Europe, and Brazil. Toyota has treated its worldwide expansion like a blueprint, with an overall vision for its growth grounded in the careful execution of hundreds, if not thousands, of small tasks.

If one is overlooked, the entire structure is weakened. Maintaining this large blueprint while focusing on the many individual parts is one way Toyota has grown from a Japanese company selling products worldwide into a true global enterprise.

Build Products Where
Products Are Sold

Toyota's philosophy is to build products regionally when volume levels warrant capital investment, and to contribute to the community as a local citizen. That is why the company, by 2008, will have the capacity to build almost two million vehicles per year in North America alone, despite the fact that only 20 years ago its capacity there was zero.

In the United States, Toyota has manufacturing facilities in San Antonio, Texas; Georgetown, Kentucky; and Princeton, Indiana, and it is, as of this writing, building a new plant in Tupelo, Mississippi. Walk down a hallway in Toyota's Motomachi manufacturing facility in Toyota City, Japan—the company's "mother plant" to the many others located across the world—and you'll see flags representing the countries where Toyota has similar factories and pictures of smiling local workers. However, each plant is allowed to develop its own identity and contribute locally to its community.

Today's situation is nothing like Toyota's approach in the 1970s. Then, the company's sales strategy, which had worked well in Japan, was to sell vehicles to customers one at a time, almost like door-to-door vacuum salesmen. In time, the company began to operate under the philosophy that cars could be sold en masse, but customers, and communities, could still be approached individually for development. Through this strategy of creating local involvement and local investment and allowing each facility to create its own identity under the more broad Toyota system, the company has flourished, selling more than $200 billion of products annually in more than 100 countries.

Consider how Toyota's role in the United States has changed over the past fifty years:

- In the 1950s and 1960s, the Big Three (General Motors, Ford, and Chrysler) produced more than 90 percent of all the vehicles in the United States.
- When Toyota first shipped vehicles to the United States in 1957, only 300 were sold.
- In 1984, Toyota sold 800,000 vehicles in the United States, but none were built domestically.
- In 1990, after opening its first U.S. factory in 1986, Toyota sold one million vehicles in the United States, earning 10 percent of the domestic market share. Many were imports.
- In 2005, 1.6 million Toyota vehicles were manufactured in the United States.
- By 2008, Toyota will have the capacity to manufacture almost two million vehicles in the United States.

Customers get much closer to a company that assumes an active stance on the local and regional level. Establishing operations is not enough; it takes building partnerships in business and the community. Toyota's massive Georgetown facility, which lies several miles outside of Louisville amid rolling hills of bluegrass and horse farms, is recognized as one of the world's best manufacturing plants. Since its opening in 1986, Toyota Motor Manufacturing Kentucky has won eight of the prestigious J.D. Power and Associates quality awards, making it one of the most decorated plants in the United States.

With roughly 7,000 employees who work together in teams of four to five, Toyota's Georgetown facility uses 700,000 square feet to produce more than 500,000 vehicles each year. It takes 20 hours to build a Camry from start to finish, with the signature Toyota Production System employed all along the way. More than 75 percent of the parts the plant uses come directly from North American suppliers, further domesticating the automaker with its "build it where you sell it" philosophy. Since the plant opened, it has returned more than $1.5 billion in tax dollars to the state of Kentucky. The company lives Samuel Smiles's imperative regarding responsibility: "The duty of helping one's self in the highest sense involves the helping of one's neighbors."

Most notable, perhaps, is Toyota's early payment of $27 million in taxes to the Scott County Board of Education. The company had financed an expansion of its Georgetown facility in 1988 with state industrial revenue bonds. Even though construction financed through such bonds is exempt from property tax, the company agreed on its own to make annual payments to the Scott County Board of Education, providing much-needed tax dollars which were not due until 2008. Also, the Georgetown operation has invested another $20-plus million dollars directly in the Kentucky area since the plant opened.

"Toyota is now accepted as part of the fabric of Kentucky," says Dennis Cuneo.

Jim Press says detractors who argue that Toyota is a foreign corporation conducting business in America need only to consider that the company has directly contributed more than $300 million in philanthropic donations in the United States, including more than $40 million per year over the last several years. Suggestions by competitors that Toyota is un-American, he says, reflect old-school thinking that does not take into account a changing landscape for global business.

"We are just like any company in America," says Press. "We are a global business in a global world. I grew up in Kansas, that's fairly American."

Toyota president Katsuaki Watanabe says the company becomes more global through regional optimization, taking into account local characteristics and circumstances. Arriving in town, setting up shop, and expecting workers to totally adapt to a Japanese company makes little business sense. So, much the way the company approached NUMMI, each new venture into a new community is intended to respect the local community and customs. The one thing Toyota works to make the same, however, is the ideal—the standard used globally by the people working to fulfill the mission of the organization. Therefore, Toyota's Japanese heritage is taken out of the equation and the emphasis is placed on learning the Toyota system as a noncultural guiding light of business.

Adapting to individual communities can be challenging. In India, for instance, Toyota faces cultural differences that are nothing like what it encounters in the United States. Indians are often quite sensitive to criticism, resisting Toyota's culture of constant improvement through problem identification, and deadlines are often not viewed with high importance. Yet the automaker has worked hard to localize its business in India, becoming as much a corporate citizen of that country as it is of any. Specifically, Toyota has invested more than $200 million in recent years through multiple joint ventures to help local suppliers become more globally competitive, and the company has worked to increase the local content of parts used in its Indian-built vehicles, becoming more of a true domestic operation.

Similarly, Toyota manufactures vehicles in France and is the only Japanese firm to manufacture vehicles in that country. The French and the Japanese have vast cultural differences, making the partnership an unlikely one. Japanese "salarymen" are known to work long hours, but in France, a 35-hour workweek prevails for most professionals. Toyota did not let this obvious problem get in the way of its principle of building products where products are sold whenever feasible and possible. Instead of just building a plant and forcing the French to adapt, Toyota found a compromise. At the Valenciennes factory, where more than 200,000 vehicles are assembled each year, employees have adopted a hybrid language mixing French and English words to make Toyota's production system a cross-cultural success. And, to further integrate the company into France, Toyota built a design center in the southern part of the country near Nice to develop cars suitable for the European market.

Most telling, though, is Toyota's decision to adapt its human resource guidelines to fit the French workers. Instead of battling the country's 35-hour workweek tradition, often perceived as an obstacle for foreign business investment, Toyota embraced it, incorporating it into planning. Today the company employs almost 4,000 people at the Valenciennes plant and has a high-profile product showroom, Le Rendez-Vous Toyota, on the Champs Elysées in Paris.

Counting subsidiaries, Toyota employs almost 300,000 world-wide; less than one-third of those, about 70,000, live in and work for the company in Japan. "To sustain growth," says Mitsuo Kinoshita, "each region needs to be self-reliant."

Toyota has set up a teaching institute in Japan for its worldwide senior employees to help foster regional and local development into the future. Years ago, when the company's employee base was largely centered in Japan, new employees learned about corporate ideals from their elders. Koki Konishi, director of the Toyota Institute, says that when he joined the company in the 1980s his superior had 42 years of experience, so he could easily see and feel Toyota's way of business. But Konishi says fast growth during the late 1990s spurred then-president Fujio Cho to create the institute, designed to serve as a kind of nerve center for global understanding.

The objective of the institute, which teaches groups of Toyota leaders from around the world throughout the year, is not to hammer in a set of rules that must be taken back home and implemented at company facilities, but to teach the corporation's way of life, so to speak, which for years has resulted in action over inaction. No matter what the local customs are, no matter how the job is best done, the Toyota Way is only about getting better every day while also contributing to the community. The institute's mission, then, is to fertilize seeds of individuality and creativity, teaching how, with Toyota's ideals, the many unique parts of the system around the world can work together to achieve common goals.

"At Toyota, a doing person is all that is needed," Konishi says. "It does not matter who they are, or where they are. We don't need geniuses. We need people willing to question, question, question. Once they find out the root cause of a problem, do it, immediately. Then disseminate and share."

13

||||||||||||||||||||||||||

Manage Like You Have No Power

If employees just did what they were told to do, you would continually find defects at the end of the line. We want employees to go
beyond what they are told and be creative, building quality into the
processes.

> —Mitsuo Kinoshita, Toyota executive vice president

TO BE A GREAT LEADER, one has to be more of a facilitator than a dictator. At many companies around the
world, including Toyota's largest competitors, bosses holding
both authority and power sit figuratively and literally high
above the employees who do the actual work. The caste system
of management places power at one level and execution at a
lower level, resulting in a frequently stifling bureaucratic quag-
mire of inefficiency due to disconnection. Those charged with
action do not fully understand either the objective or the consequences; they are merely following orders. Likewise, the ones
holding the power are far too removed from the actual work to
understand the import or effectiveness of their orders.

Consider a typical family with school-age children. In a caste system structure, in which the parent maintains all power, ordering a child to do his or her homework does not give the parent control over whether the homework gets done or not. Action lies solely in the hands of the child. Often the directive will be enough to get the homework done; if it isn't, no amount of nagging will improve the end result.

Now, reflect back on what happened at Ford several years ago under the leadership of then-chairman and CEO Bill Ford Jr., the great-grandson of company founder Henry Ford. Few corporate leaders in America over the years have been as affable and articulate in vision as Bill Ford. Despite being the company's richest employee during his tenure, Ford displayed an understanding of the need for drastic cost cutting. He talked at length publicly about the automaker's need to be a leader in environmentally friendly vehicles, and he spoke of a future in which the company contributed mightily to a better world. Even some of the most jaded automotive journalists and observers agreed that Ford's leadership stance made perfect sense.

Unfortunately, Bill Ford's stance remained an ideal and little more than a directive to the company's 100,000-plus employees. At Ford, those charged with execution were frequently doing one thing while the company leader was saying another. Traditionally one of the most bureaucratic of the world's largest corporations, Ford Motor Company is emblematic of what happens when the people and the system get bigger than the entity and its goals: Decision making is slow and rigid as information must travel through mazes of approval and bureaucracy. How else could a once-strong company like Ford, which had more than $140 billion in sales in 2006 and a vast turnaround plan, lose more than $12 billion in a single year of operations?

After several years of valiant effort, Bill Ford realized his plans were not working. Alan Mulally was brought on from Boeing to tackle the unenviable task of rebuilding the company. Among Mulally's first tasks on the job: arranging a meeting in Japan with Toyota chairman Fujio Cho. Calling Toyota "the finest machine in the world, the finest production system in the world," Mulally says he traveled abroad early in his automotive leadership tenure to "study the master"—Toyota. The meeting, interestingly, completed a full circle of learning that began with Kiichiro Toyoda studying Ford and its lean production decades earlier.

Among the valuable lessons Mulally learned was that Toyota became the world's best automaker on the strength of a management system that encourages leaders to empower team members to think and act on their own. Conversely, the culture at Ford, said top executive Mark Fields, has been one of equating a request for help with weakness. Directives come down from on-high, and lower-level employees are simply expected to do their jobs, no questions asked. Never mind that the order may be misguided; team members are not empowered to explore a different direction even if instinct and experience shows it to be a better way.

So, as Ford continued to spiral downward under the weight of its inefficient structure, Toyota's steady ascent marked by stability, growth, and evolution continued on the strength of a management structure that empowers employees, turning managers and leaders more into facilitators and coaches than bosses and autocrats. With strong and empowered employees, the organization strengthens considerably. Toyota executive vice president Mitsuo Kinoshita, who, among his many roles oversees global human resources, compares it to a stone wall surrounding a well-known Japanese castle. The wall, he says, is comprised of stones of various sizes—some large, some small. Regardless of size, though, each stone is important, supporting the others. Small stones support big stones, and vice versa. Together, they build a powerful wall. If management takes the power away from smaller stones, though, the structure will ultimately collapse.

Distribute Authority Widely

Few executives in corporate management have more respect from and authority with employees than Toyota's Gary Convis, the company's leading North American manufacturing executive before retiring in 2007 to become a senior executive adviser. Tall, fit, energetic, and following an automotive career that took him from General Motors to NUMMI to Toyota, he could easily operate as a dictating leader at Toyota's manufacturing plants, finding many team members who would enthusiastically follow his orders. But after earning one of the most coveted manufacturing jobs in the industry—executive vice president of Toyota North America—Convis was taught one of his most valuable management lessons by his Japanese supervisor, a company executive vice president.

With expanded duties—from managing Toyota's Georgetown plant to overseeing all of Toyota's manufacturing facilities in North America—Convis was told by his superior to avoid being a dictatorial boss and to manage as if he had no power. *Manage as if he had no power.* Predictably, Convis was caught off guard by the advice, despite being well-versed in Toyota's philosophy of coaching employees and teaching them to help themselves so that they can ultimately help the company. The concept goes against everything many corporate executives are about—namely, having and *using* power and authority. Getting his biggest career promotion and receiving instructions to manage as if he had no power caused Convis to give pause.

"I thought, 'My goodness—what an amazing approach,'" says Convis. "And I thought, would a North American executive in a similar type of business ever say that to a newly promoted person? Never. So I've never forgotten that."

In reflection, Convis says the profound statement rang true with his management beliefs and what he had been learning from the Toyota Way during his years with the company. He recognized that his success thus far at Toyota had been cultivated in the very same way, with superiors who managed as if they had no power, unleashing him as a primary source of continuous improvement and change. He recalls multiple instances when those above him placed decision-making authority in his hands. In one example, Convis went to a superior to get sign-off on a relatively large capital expenditure for the Georgetown plant. Convis had researched the need and presented the findings to his boss. The superior, ultimately responsible for the decision, told Convis to make the decision himself and come back to him not with a request for approval but with a recommendation.

"It turned the worm on me," says Convis. "It made me think, 'I'd better check again.' It teaches you to not reach an opinion, but to get the facts; all of the facts."

Even today, in a position of high authority at Toyota—*especially* today in a position of high authority at Toyota—Convis, as well as fellow senior managers, are challenged, if not prodded, to act not as a boss but as a facilitator who is also actively involved in problem solving for the company. In other words, even though Convis has become a coach, he must remain willing to learn, to leave ego out of the equation, and to maintain a willingness to personally "go and see" to determine facts and ensure that viable decisions are made. When meeting with Toyota's formidable 26-member board of directors in Japan, he and other managing officers continue to experience *namawashi*, the hashing out of pros and cons of every subject so truth is revealed, with facts always ruling over popular opinion.

Toyota's way is not based on a company being run on the popular whims of one; instead, it runs on the amalgamated fact-based platforms formed by groups of people. In senior meetings, questions are posed professionally, in the humble way of Toyota, but participants are expected to avoid conjecture, hearsay, and unsubstantiated opinion and be prepared to present facts or go back to the source for more research. Such an approach is more powerful than aggressive or condescending questioning, says Convis, considering that at Toyota expectations run high for preparedness and more authority often means more responsibility. As a result, even though he is a high-level executive for one of the world's most effective companies, direct challenges from superiors of his fact-based findings never cease.

"On our board of directors," says Convis, ". . . there is not a lot of homocentric thinking. It is not about opinion. Decisions are fact-based . . . go and see and obtain a deep understanding. Then we expose weaknesses. At some point visionary leaders have to sign off on it, but everyone is challenged to find the answers. I have never left a meeting with [fellow Toyota executives and board members] without them challenging me to improve and take this company to the next level."

In conversations with Toyota employees and top executives, one quickly learns that the word "I" rarely comes up. Instead, the most-used term is "we," and it does not come off as a scripted public relations ploy but as a matter of fact, reflecting Toyota's team-based structure. Because employees are encouraged to share information, and because higher-ranking employees are encouraged to serve as mentors of lower-level employees, Toyota has a more horizontal organizational structure. Another key component of this configuration is the matrix structure employed for some aspects of the company, in which all employees who do one type of work, like engineering, are put in a pool in order to work with several managers from different departments. So while traditional, hierarchical management is prevalent throughout the organization, the matrix structure concept is applied to generate responsibility from the bottom up.

Toyota's use of the matrix structure in engineering gives the company significant advantage over competitors in product development because multiple people working together are empowered with "responsibility without authority"—challenged to uncover truths, find solutions, and contribute as stakeholders of the project of the moment. As Jeffrey Liker explains in his book *The Toyota Way*, "formal authority" at Toyota "is typically one level up from responsibility," meaning that the person responsible, who in reality is not the boss or superior, must function as an empowered decision-maker. Just as Convis's superior refused to merely sign off on a large expenditure and instructed Convis to take responsibility for the decision, each Toyota employee is called to "defend his or her ideas, work through other people, and convince the person with formal authority that the ideas are correct."

In engineering, the chief engineer is seen as the most powerful of all employees in product development, but in reality he or she does not have more than a handful of direct reports. In a typical American corporate structure, a manager with just six direct reports would never be one of the most influential and powerful employees in a large company, but at Toyota, the opposite is often true. Chief engineers are responsible for vehicle program development, serving as the authorities, but they are not directly responsible for most of the team members who have the responsibility for getting the job done.

The matrix system has several advantages. Because employees are not isolated into internal cliques, information is more easily shared across functions, and the workload shifts faster across a more flexible workforce. Also, the organization allows for employees to have much more broad-based knowledge because they are not focused on one boss and one task. Opponents of a matrix structure might argue that having multiple bosses and working on multiple projects causes confusion, but Toyota's record in engineering and product development speaks for itself. Different levels of a matrix system exist in other areas of Toyota as well, most notably in manufacturing.

The structure is one way Toyota keeps bureaucracy at bay as it becomes one of the largest corporate enterprises in the world. Gary Convis, for instance, says he has never had just one boss during his time at Toyota and still does not today, even though he sits on the company's board of managing executives. The structure is similar to a village raising a child. A flourishing, active child may answer to a parent or parents at home but likely also answers to teachers, coaches, and maybe even neighbors or grandparents who contribute daily to the child's ongoing management and instruction. Some days, the child spends more time with one authority; other days, he or she spends more time with another. Ultimately, though, the child has the responsibility to do the work, whatever the task may be.

At Toyota, the system is one of cascading goals in which the aims of the company take center stage. The organization's objectives and leadership foster teamwork and take the "I" and "me" out of the equation. Responsibility drops one level below authority and authority is distributed so employees work for common goals rather than for one single authoritarian figure. Outside the manufacturing plant, Toyota relies on a traditional pyramid structure with executives, managers, and team members, but a horizontal system is fully in play each day as processes are designed to encourage information flow and remove barriers. Having managers work in open offices with employees makes them more accessible while also allowing them to readily participate in the daily work flow. It helps, as well, that the company's continual emphasis on going to the source forces managers and executives to drop down one or more levels in fact finding, further reducing barriers to productivity and effective execution.

Strive for Lean, Avoid Bureaucracy

Toyota's management system is rooted in the company's philosophy of finding ways to achieve more with less. The study of other corporations, dating back to Kiichiro Toyoda's examination of Ford, has taught Toyota leaders that an organization characterized by bureaucracy and impersonal decision making in a pyramid-style hierarchy is wasteful. Excessively tall managements systems, like those used by General Motors, Ford, and Chrysler, often confine employees to their specialization, preventing them from using the flexibility that would help them achieve greater goals and objectives. Such top-down management often results in a system where orders are given by executives who may have a good idea of what to do but who have no control over what really gets done.

As we've seen, Toyota's bottom-up empowerment turns the company's management into something closer to "coordinators" than bosses. Their chief responsibility is to coach employees on how to work together and continually find ways to improve. Yuki Funo, chairman and CEO of Toyota Motor Sales USA, is a living example of Toyota's management philosophy. Of the thousands of American employees, he is the only one who rises in authority above other managers.

Toyota's horizontal system applies not just to employees but to different company divisions as well. Typically, large global companies set up their divisions on different continents as a series of minipyramids operating under one larger pyramid. In other words, a company's main corporate operations would be "taller" than its main operations for North America, but North American operations would have its own tall structure with level commands. That is how Ford and General Motors operate in Europe, with relatively autonomous foreign operations that are run by a head authority responsible to global headquarters. Toyota's system views such structure as bureaucratic and instead uses a decidedly more lateral flow of both reporting and responsibility.

Toyota Motor Sales USA, for instance, is one entity, but it is not *the* entity in America. The division is called to work directly with other U.S. divisions, such as manufacturing and engineering, but the division does not hold ruling authority over any other divisions in the United States. Toyota Motor Sales

USA, the Georgetown, Kentucky, manufacturing plant, and Toyota's American engineering offices all report directly to Toyota's global headquarters, resulting in a horizontal structure designed to fight the ills of excessive layering and vertical management structures.

Contrast that system with the one at General Motors. According to company chairman Robert Lutz, during product development initiatives, "each of its four global operations would have brought cars to life on its own, like four eggs in separate frying pans that never connected." And yet, many Toyota opponents claim the primary reasons GM struggles to effectively compete with the Japanese automakers are:

1. Health-care and legacy costs.
2. Toyota's currency advantages because of Japan's control of the yen value, creating significant exchange benefits.

Also, Toyota's health-care and pension expense is only a fraction of GM's, as low as a couple of hundred dollars per vehicle. And, nobody can deny that since the central bank of Japan began spending billions around 2001 buying U.S. Treasury bonds and other dollar assets to keep the value of the yen in check, Toyota has benefited considerably.

However, while these are undeniably inhibiting business factors, they still don't explain why General Motors has not been able to adapt or become more flexible in its management approach. To be the best, you have to be lean and less bureaucratic, solve problems rather than just cite excuses. At Toyota, even the dealer network is smaller in the effort to remain lean and keep bureaucracy at bay. At the end of 2006, for instance, General Motors had more than 7,000 dealers in the United

States for its brands, which accounted for a 25 percent market share, while Toyota had just more than 1,200 dealers in the United States for its brands, commanding roughly 15 percent of the market. With a smaller dealer network, communication with the sales network is streamlined and Toyota is able to instill core principles due to the less bureaucratic, lean structure which effectively empowers the partners.

14

||||||||||||||||||||||||||||

Carefully Cultivate and Support Partners

We begin to create the culture in the hiring process.

—Gary Convis, senior executive adviser for Toyota

THE TRADITION IN JAPANESE BUSINESS has long been to hire candidates who best fit the company, rather than to hire on resumé alone. After a year of evaluation and training, companies then assign new hires to the appropriate jobs. The practice takes the emphasis off specific skills, instead identifying employees who fit well within a company's culture. For Toyota, a company deeply rooted in its culture, this hiring method works well, enabling it to find new employees who respect people and are willing to improve on the job.

Despite Toyota's rapid, global growth over the past two decades, the company has not abandoned its extensive, hands-on training program for new hires in its home country. The time-tested program thoroughly teaches both the business and the culture through varied, in-the-field experiences. Orientation for Toyota's new white-collar hires in Japan typically lasts for one year. It includes three months working in the factory, rotating through different jobs so employees can learn about all aspects of Toyota's unique manufacturing process. New hires are then sent to work in Toyota dealerships to learn about the sales process and the customer. In essence, a Japanese Toyota employee's first year is part of a complex apprenticeship in continuous improvement and respect for people. It begins the first day on the job and goes on for several years, until the new hire becomes a fully trained, experienced employee able to teach others. This is consistent with Samuel Smiles's vision of how one should be trained: "The apprenticeship of difficulty is one which the greatest of men have had to serve," he wrote.

Once placed by human resources in a specific department, each new hire is assigned an experienced mentor within the company with whom they work closely for three years, discussing everything from job-related problems, to company traditions and practices, to expectations and opportunities. While the mentors' role is partly to support the new hires, they also push their protégés out of their comfort zones when appropriate, helping them to grow and make progress. While visiting, this journalist had the opportunity to interview a Toyota new hire whose English was minimal at best. The employee's mentor had arranged the interview. The new hire was uncomfortable speaking without a translator and fidgeted as he struggled to answer questions about the mentor program. Later, the mentor explained that she wanted him to understand the importance of improving his English.

The apprenticeship program for new hires stems from Japan's jobs-for-life tradition. Following a decade of stagnant economic growth, many Japanese companies no longer strictly abide by the jobs-for-life practice, finding themselves forced to make layoffs. Toyota no longer strictly adheres to the principle, either, but for different reasons. Because Toyota often needs more experienced professionals, more midcareer hires are being brought into the company. Still, Toyota has not backed off its extensive training and mentoring program, believing that properly prepared employees are necessary to support the company's long-term philosophy. If anything, Toyota continues to improve its careful hiring process and extensive training and mentoring program.

Reinforce Culture Through Deep and Thorough Teaching

The support of Toyota's employees begins at the company's highest level. According to Toyota's philosophy of respect, all employees are called upon to help one another and share their knowledge and experience, whether it's in their job descriptions or not. That is why company president Katsuaki Watanabe teaches at the Toyota Institute, as does executive vice president Mitsuo Kinoshita.

"Toyota executives are 100 percent interested in human resource development," says institute director Koki Konishi. "They believe it is their job . . . not their responsibility, but their fate . . . the fate of the company."

To expand employee cultivation and training as the company grows overseas, mentor programs are being established in the United States and Asia, as are some of the extensive problem-solving seminars that Japanese employees undergo. While non-Japanese employees may not receive a year in training or be required to work in the factory, Toyota exposes key professional employees to its manufacturing principles through training at its University of Toyota, a training ground in California.

"We want to have an environment," says Mitsuo Kinoshita, "where the supervisor teaches. We cannot do in each environment exactly what we want to do. We have to adapt. But, this culture of teaching and being taught is important to Toyota. The principle remains the same wherever we are."

Teaching and mentoring is so important at Toyota, in fact, that one's ability to teach and mentor is a key factor in employee appraisal. Jim Press's and Gary Convis's ability to articulate the qualities and principles of the Toyota Way is no accident. Conversely, the American executives became leaders within the company in part because they understand the value of sharing knowledge and have the ability to communicate with employees at all levels and across all functions of the organization.

Strategically, Toyota's human resource approach has been a significant weapon that has helped to fuel its success over the years. As competitors like General Motors, Ford, Chrysler, and Nissan experience attrition due mostly to layoffs, Toyota has advanced with a stable workforce that fully understands the guiding corporate principles. Into the future, this human resource gap among competitors should only widen as Toyota increases its training while its competitors continue to lose valuable experience. Conducting mentor programs would be next to impossible today at Ford, for example, since more than one-third of its experienced white-collar employees have left the company in the past several years.

Toyota, on the other hand, maintains its experience through its sustainability and by seeking out new team members who best reflect the principles of the company's operating philosophy, which include practicality, inquisitiveness, reverence, a desire to improve, and the passion to contribute to the welfare of people and community. Whether or not the prospective employee is a student of Toyota or of lean production, or a leading expert in a chosen field, does not matter as much as certain intangibles. It's more important that he or she possess a desire to succeed, commit, and remain open-minded in finding new and better ways of doing business. The approach is different from many companies that hire the most talented people, expecting them to fit into the culture after the fact.

Since Toyota's philosophy is a mind-set designed to unleash employee creativity and contribution rather than a collection of specific tools and traditions, employees cannot be expected to join the company with any real goals other than wanting to contribute. In its hiring process, Toyota does not look for understanding so much as for willingness. The idea is not to simply get the right team in place and let them decide where to go. The only aspects constant in Toyota's business principles are its mission: continuous improvement and respect for people. The issue thus becomes more about *how* than *where*.

Thus willingness to learn is among the more necessary traits for obtaining a job at Toyota, since people can be taught the Toyota Production System more easily than they can be taught to admit they do not know how to do something. An individual with a rebellious mind-set has no place at Toyota, a company where the suggestion that a process or function cannot be improved equates to an act of treason. According to Toyota's principles, every aspect of business, or life, no matter how refined it may seem, can be improved. Hiring managers also look closely for honesty and integrity in prospective employees, since the culture relies heavily upon service above self and a willingness to be critiqued.

Says Jim Press, "People either have it or they don't. Either you are a part of it or you are not. For many, it is a fertile ground. . . . People that don't have it, they try, then they usually end up leaving because they know."

But for those employees who connect with Toyota's system and principles, who find the one-of-a-kind way of conducting business redeeming, the opportunities for learning never cease. They also receive strong leadership from members of the founding Toyoda family in Japan. It is rare to find a company, which has grown so large in such a short span of time—from the small regional loom sales in the 1930s to the global annual automotive sales in 2007 exceeding $200 billion—that remains so intimately connected to its founding fathers. Toyota's strength is that the Toyoda family, now led by Dr. Shoichiro Toyoda, has remained a pillar of respectability and guidance.

To explain the connection of employees hired at Toyota today to the ideals of the founding family, Press recalls an old science-fiction television show in which a planet was discovered where inhabitants had maintained an unchanging culture for 600 years. The reason turns out to be a brainlike center—an old satellite still transmitting repetitive signals. Similarly, says Press, as the world changes and the company adapts into the twenty-first century, Dr. Toyoda and the Toyoda family are still around and very active as a corporate nerve center.

"The signal is still being transmitted," says Press.

On the job, employees typically find the company to be thorough in training but forgiving of mistakes. Once hired, remaining in good standing is said to be relatively easy, as long as employees come to work and continue to exhibit the traits that singled them out for employment in the first place. Mistakes, as previously noted, are viewed by Toyota as learning opportunities, as long as team members are quick to point them out. Frequently, says Gary Convis, mistakes are not the team member's fault, anyway, but the result of faulty instructions, especially when new employees are involved. If the worker has not learned, he says, the teacher has not taught.

"We do not accept shipping something beyond the workspace that is not perfect," says Convis. "We know what person is on what job, and our brand image and the reputation of the whole company rest on that trust. We can forgive people for mistakes but we need somebody with honesty and integrity to show up and be willing to speak up when there's a problem."

As stated earlier, manufacturing employees at Toyota face essentially just two primary job demands:

1) Come to work everyday.
2) Pull the cord when there's a problem.

Because Toyota does not use labor pools, punctuality is a necessity. If one team member is absent in manufacturing, the team leader has to fill in. This setup varies greatly from that of U.S. automakers, where the union covers absentees with fill-in workers, going so far as to prescribe off-time for members struggling on the job or with personal issues. Also, making problems visible can be intimidating for many until they become confident and comfortable with the system.

"For Americans and anyone, it can be a shock to the system to be actually expected to make problems visible," said

Latondra Newton, a thirty-eight-year-old Indiana native who works at Toyota Motor Engineering & Manufacturing North America, Inc., in Erlanger, Kentucky. "Other corporate environments tend to hide problems from bosses."

In addition, Toyota team members are taught to take mutual ownership of problems identified by others. Making a problem visible does no good if all the available talent does not work together to quickly solve it. Taking the attitude that a company problem falling directly under the auspices of another employee is only "their problem" is not only self-serving and against Toyota's principles, it is also damaging to the overall strength of the enterprise. In Toyota's workplace, the problems of one are believed to be the problems of all, since waste in the smallest increments can inflict significant damage on the larger entity.

Seek Mutual Benefit

Toyota's cooperative relationship with workers dates back to the defining moment in the early 1950s when the company lost money and was forced to make layoffs. Toyota's leadership met with labor leaders, and both groups agreed they wanted to do whatever possible to make sure such strain did not occur again. The parties agreed to establish a formal program of trust and negotiation in which all concerns are openly and honestly discussed until a solution with mutual benefit is reached.

Toyota and the labor leaders established a congenial method for negotiating wages and benefits each year, one that carefully considers the needs of both labor and management and the ultimate goal of contributing to society. As a result, Toyota has gone for over 50 years without so much as a threat of a strike and without the adversarial relationship that so often hurts American automakers. Today, Kinoshita says, Toyota executives and managers frequently look back to that historic agreement when making decisions in partnerships.

"It is one of the strengths of Toyota," he says. "We do not rush to reach conclusion. We listen and work together to reach common understanding."

By applying the same principles to supplier relationships, Toyota has also been able to gain significant advantage over competitors year after year. When purchasing parts, for instance, Toyota does not simply order suppliers to lower costs and suffer the consequences. Instead, the company conducts a cost analysis, then works closely with the supplier to reduce costs when necessary, searching for solutions that benefit both parties. Because Toyota works to make sure its suppliers remain both profitable and viable with the win-win relationship approach, trust between the partners remains high—which is unusual in the global automotive industry.

The foundation of Toyota relationships, according to executive vice president Mitsuo Kinoshita:

1. Establish mutual trust.
2. Mutually improve productivity and share the benefits.
3. Mutually contribute to the betterment of society and economy.

15

||||||||||||||||||||||||||||

The Power of Paranoia

I feel that being successful may make us arrogant and want to stay in a comfort zone. That is the threat.

—Katsuaki Watanabe, president, Toyota Motor Corporation

IF RESPECT IS TOYOTA'S LIFEBLOOD, then worry is its beating heart—the relentlessly pumping force that keeps driving the enterprise to greater and greater heights. The more the company achieves, reaching all-time profits and overtaking competitors, the more the company's culture makes it fear that what is being done today is not good enough for tomorrow.

Sure, the automaker earned billions the year before, but costs in the same period rose; yes, the company was highly rated for initial product quality, but defects numbered in the hundreds of thousands; admittedly, Toyota has passed competitors, but that advantage cannot be taken for granted. Listen to executives long enough and you'll be convinced Toyota is not one of the greatest corporations in the world but one of the *worst*. Beginning at the top of the company with president Katsuaki Watanabe, nurtured by the executive board, and spread infectiously throughout the rest of the corporation, worry is a way of life at Toyota: "We always plan for the worst and hope for the best," says Jim Press.

To become the best, you must become convinced that failure is the enemy, a threat manifested in complacency, waste, arrogance, and misplaced focus. No matter how effusively the world praises Toyota in its position of global leadership, Watanabe refuses to pay attention, adhering to the traditional Toyota belief that no matter how good some people say you are, the truth is never as flattering as the press clippings.

Aside from product praise, bold, boastful talk from Toyota is relatively nonexistent. Instead, the company worries about weaknesses in quality and efficiency and burgeoning bureaucracy, which Watanabe fears will put Toyota on a path of mediocrity if not properly addressed. "There are grounds for concern," Toyota's president said in late 2006, as the world began to recognize that Toyota was zooming toward a global leadership role.

The ever-present fear of failure, of course, is one of the innate traits that have made all the difference for Toyota during its decades-long continual rise in efficiency, service, strength, and power. When Toyota first planned to manufacture products in the United States in the 1980s, leaders worried endlessly that what worked so well in Japan could not be duplicated. The company put unprecedented effort into carefully instilling the Toyota Production System at its first American factory. When Toyota became poised to leap past Ford and General Motors to become the world's largest automaker, simultaneously obliterating its competitors in terms of profits, growth, and customer satisfaction, Toyota leaders began to worry that the company might never be the same again.

"They worry about details. They never stop worrying," says David Cole, chairman of the Center for Automotive Research in Ann Arbor, Michigan, in regard to Toyota's leadership. "They encourage worrying in the company, from the top down."

If the company became satisfied with being the front-runner and showed arrogance, it would be abandoning the very qualities that allowed Toyota to become the best and biggest automaker in the world in the first place. Toyota's "fear first, plan for the worst, hope for the best" mantra fits with its problems-first culture. Continuous improvement becomes difficult when risks and inhibiting factors are not thoroughly assessed and understood. Translation: Running scared yields better results than running complacent. To win the race, it helps to feel the whole pack is after you and many obstacles block the way.

"Everyone should be dissatisfied with the present situation and should constantly try to improve or change things," says Watanabe. "It's important to realize that there is always something more we need to aim at. That's what needs to be recognized by every individual. When you're growing you're satisfied with the status quo, and that's no good."

Exercise Great Caution

In late 2006, news reached the mainstream media of a Toyota internal report stating that if the company did not hold down costs in the United States, its profitable future would be threatened. For those unfamiliar with Toyota's culture of worry, this report probably seemed curiously ill-timed, considering that arguably no other manufacturing company had posted such sterling, across-the-board results for one year of operation as Toyota had in 2006. If anything, it seemed like Toyota should be toasting its own success, taking time to enjoy its record profits, robust sales growth, and unlimited opportunity as the world's top carmaker. Another company might have reveled in the moment by doling out record bonuses and celebrating its great year.

Just consider what Toyota competitor Ford did after the company lost more than $12 billion in 2006. The company, interestingly, handed out millions of dollars in executive and employee bonuses in early 2007 for the previous year's work, despite the record losses. (Originally the bonuses were just slated for executives, but negativity in the media and on Internet chat boards led to a change and all employees were included in the handout.)

What was Toyota's leadership doing as 2006 came to a close? With long-term strategy primarily driving all actions and fear running deep amongst company leaders, Toyota was at work—during its best fiscal year ever—planning for the problems that it forecasted to plague its future—namely, rising wages and benefits at American manufacturing plants. Citing a "high-level company report" from Seiichi (Sean) Sudo, president of Toyota Engineering and Manufacturing in the United States, the *Detroit Free Press* in early 2007 noted internal concern at the automaker that personnel costs were growing at a rate faster than profits, posing a serious threat to the company's future. Because the report projected "a $900 million increase in U.S. manufacturing compensation" in the next decade—resulting, according to Sudo, in "a condition that is not sustainable"—the recommendation was reportedly made for Toyota to reduce future benefits and wages in the United States by tying them more closely to regions and avoiding the traditional pay received by union automotive workers in the Detroit area.

Unaffordable labor and benefit costs, after all, have been cited over the years by leaders at GM, Ford, and Chrysler as leading factors in their companies' struggles. If Toyota should follow the same path, allowing future expenses to grow faster than profits, it could end up another also-ran of tomorrow, a giant, inflexible, bureaucratic machine bound in the future by its frivolous past. So, Toyota executives remain worried and vigilant in the best of times. If the company can attract skilled workers in Mississippi by offering $20 an hour, for instance, and that wage is higher than what other companies in the area are paying, why would Toyota pay workers $28 an hour just to match what Ford's union employees are earning in Michigan?

The fact that America's domestic automakers have not aggressively tackled plaguing wage and benefit problems renders those companies, as one pundit said in 2006, little more than pension plans that occasionally turn out vehicles. The objective for Toyota, says Jim Press, is to find employees who share the same ideals of long-term vision and short-term vigilance, creating a win-win scenario. Yes, he says, many employees of GM, Ford, and Chrysler earn slightly more than Toyota employees. But, he argues, compare how many American jobs those corporations have eliminated in recent years (tens of thousands) with how many American jobs Toyota has created (thousands). Besides, he says, Toyota typically pays the highest wages in the areas where its plants are located. Employees who

Says Press:

- Approach your job from the perspective that good news can wait.
- Ask yourself: What can we do to get better?
- Avoid complacency.
- Come to work every day like it is your first.

approach the job in the spirit of Toyota's principles, he says, should have no problem prospering well into the future.

Don't Believe the Headlines

If winning in the global marketplace seems easy for Toyota, Don Esmond wants to set the record straight. He says nothing Toyota has achieved in terms of market share and customer satisfaction, particularly in the United States, has been easy. From the start, according to Esmond, it has been a struggle. First, there was the Toyopet, the company's American product entry that consumers never warmed up to, seeing it as little more than a Japanese car exported to the United States. Then there was the stigma associated with being a foreign automaker. In the late 1970s, American autoworkers bashed Japanese cars on television in protest of the competitive threat as consumers increasingly turned to the smaller, more efficient cars.

The American media largely ignored Toyota, instead more closely covering the product launches and activities of the domestic automakers even though the Japanese company was increasingly becoming a primary choice for millions of consumers. It did not matter that since the early 1990s Toyota's products were widely considered to be better and less costly on both the front end and the back end due to lower service costs. Not until Toyota passed Ford in size and began to make a run at General Motors to become the world's largest automaker did the media really stand up and take note of the growing threat from the East.

No longer viewed as just a manufacturing enigma worthy of high-level business study, the company by late 2006 and continuing into 2007 made one media headline after another. Stories ranging from predictions of just how far Toyota could go in its global endeavor, to how the company trains new employees, to how competitors have virtually no chance of competing against the automaker in the twenty-first century were delivered rapid fire.

Headlines included:

"From Zero to 60 to World Domination" (*New York Times Magazine*)
"A Carmaker Wired to Win" (*Business Week*)
"Toyota Takes No. 1 Spot from GM" (*Detroit Free Press*)

At many companies, such glowing headlines would be cause for celebration, evidence of hard work and good fortune. But Don Esmond, Katsuaki Watanabe, and others at Toyota feel the challenge is more difficult today than ever before. When the Toyopet flopped in America, Toyota's leaders had only a single product with minimal presence to worry about. Now Toyota has billions invested in infrastructure in the United States and dozens of other countries around the world, and the challenge is infinitely more daunting.

If anything, during the finest moment in Toyota's history, worry has reached an all-time high, with the growing attention becoming yet another cause for concern. For decades the company had operated in relative obscurity, considering the size of the company and its global breadth to build and sell cars around the world. Because most of its operations in Japan were located in a more remote area of the country, hours from Tokyo, and because company leaders never positioned themselves above the brand, story lines leaned more toward basic news reporting. Toyota was allowed to fly below the radar. Even in Detroit, many journalists have been amazed at how little executives at General Motors and Ford talked about Toyota. They obsessed about one another but rarely mentioned Toyota.

All that changed when Toyota finally emerged on the radar screen in a big way. The company's leaders feared backlash, worrying its success might cause some competitors and media to see the company in a different light and take a more aggressive approach with the former-underdog-turned-marketplace-leader. In response, Toyota became more visible, particularly in the United States. The commercials for the new full-size truck were more direct and bold than usual for the company's products; Toyota made a high profile entry into NASCAR; and Americans got to see Jim Press swimming on the *Today* show.

The idea, says Press, is to not sit back, getting clobbered, tackling hearsay with fact. He says he was embarrassed when

Toyota's formula for excellence:

- Maintain strong principles.
- Constantly change.
- Don't believe the headlines along the way.

the feature on NBC's *Today* show focused on his swimming, because he would prefer people talk about the company's products rather than his breaststroke. And in the Toyota tradition, Press worries the attention will only lead to more problems. The company has much to offer more people, Press says, so he understands the story needs to be accurately told, but he still has a litany of concerns for the future.

CONCLUSION

||||||||||||||||||||||||||||||||||||||||||||||||||||

Work for the Right Reasons

Our goal is to . . . make life easier.

—Jim Press, president, Toyota Motor North America

FROM THE MOMENT SAKICHI TOYODA passed his principles for business on to his son Kiichiro in the early 1920s, he ignited a powerful concept that would evolve into the strong multinational corporation it would eventually become. Company leaders recall discussing how Toyota might one day emerge as one of the world's larger and most important companies, but most admit they never expected it to happen so fast.

By sticking to the same principles for more than eight decades while constantly changing and upgrading the specific methods and processes, Toyota has made steady and substantial progress since the 1950s. Because the company remained grounded in humility, listening to the customer without arrogance and striving to make a positive contribution to its community and the larger world, Toyota finds itself in the twenty-first century faced with enormous opportunity and responsibility.

Jim Press, for one, says he is not surprised it happened. When Toyota quietly invested more than $1 billion in the early 1990s in patented hybrid technology to build a car for the future, for example, nobody paid much attention. But as the world begins to acknowledge the possibility of future fossil fuel shortages and the potential damage being done to the global environment by automotive emissions, Toyota's years of dedication to "providing clean and safe products" and fostering a culture that "enhances individual creativity" have led Toyota to the top of the global car industry. The efficient cars that met customer needs in the fuel-conscious 1970s; the luxury Lexus cars that established the company's reputation for quality and innovation; the game-changing Camry; the world-changing Prius: all contributed to providing Toyota a competitive advantage that would help it become the leader in the intensely competitive automobile market.

"Things accelerated faster than we thought," says Press, "but does anybody think 50 years from today it will not be any different?"

Press suggests that Toyota's global leadership comes "at the right place, at the right time"—part happenstance and part hard work—after years of striving to do the right things and improve performance bit by bit. Today the company's only choice is to stick to the company principles like never before as the challenge becomes infinitely harder. Toyota's leadership must remember that the financials are never the means, they are the result—the end product of doing all the things that have gotten them this far.

Jim Press says doing the right thing at the office each day requires little more than asking simple questions:

- How can we best serve customers?
- How fulfilled are employees?
- How are we contributing to quality of life?
- What is our impact on the environment?

Cynics will say that Toyota's talk of working for the right reasons and caring so much about society and the environment is little more than a public relations ploy to fend off any backlash as the company's profits soar. They will argue that such talk is mere lip service for a company that now earns more money than several of its competitors combined. That, however, is exactly the point.

Throughout Toyota's rise, its leaders have not apologized for the company's profitability. As a publicly traded company, Toyota has obligations to its shareholders and employees. Profit, also, is essential for sustainability, the ultimate result sought from Toyota's core principles of continuous improvement and respect for people. By doing the right things daily, the company grows profitably while serving more and more customers around the globe.

Profit becomes the pleasing end result of doing the right things. Neither is size a corporate objective, according to company president Watanabe: "Sales volume and market share are not important," he says. The man known for his cost-cutting and quality initiatives has a much larger vision for the future. His dream car will be able to drive cross-country on one tank of gas, cleaning the air as it goes. What's more, Watanabe says, the company is working to build cars that use sensor warning systems to save passengers from collisions. The ultimate objective, he says, is building cars that actually improve consumers' lives in every conceivable way. Says Watanabe, "For us to become the genuine number one—in quality—we have to realize the dream vehicle which makes the air cleaner, never injures people, makes people healthier, and can run on a single tank of fuel between London and Istanbul."

If such ambitions sound far-fetched, remember that in the 1920s Toyota was still only a loom company. The first car had not yet been imagined. Today, the Toyota Group, which stands on the principle of making the world better by building things, builds "luxury and comfort" housing in Japan. It is also in the marine business, building pleasure boats and engines, and it is using its financial services arm to build "customers for life" by financing everything from housing and cars to pleasure boats and consumer loans.

However, Toyota's primary business—automotive design, manufacturing, sales, and service—still holds the most promise and the most opportunity for contributing to society in the years ahead. The mission becomes important not only for Toyota, but also for the industry as well, as many of the world's largest automakers find themselves in dire straits early in the twenty-first century.

As Toyota soared to the top, most were struggling just to hang on. Amid billions of dollars in losses in 2006, Ford offered buyouts to employees in an effort to eliminate thousands of jobs, and some 8,000 more than expected took the offer. General Motors eliminated the jobs of more than 30,000 workers over several years, and Chrysler announced in early 2007 that 13,000 workers would lose their jobs in a massive restructuring as profits dwindled amid lagging sales. Sales at each of America's Big Three are stagnant, and the turmoil comes at perhaps at the most important growth period facing the global automotive industry. Toyota forecasts that the number of cars on the roads in the world will more than double in the next decade. Press says that in America alone 64 million young people will receive driver's licenses in the next 10 years. He does not, therefore, see Toyota's ascension in global business size and strength as a pinnacle but an opportunity. The challenges today are greater than ever before, Press says, and Toyota's principles are more important than ever before.

"If you get to the top of the mountain, you keep climbing," he says. "As long as [Toyota] continues to focus on the heart of the customer, remaining true to the mission of working to improve society, [it] can keep this going."

APPENDIX A

||||||||||||||||||||||||||||||||||||||||||||

Toyota's Guiding Principles

1. Honor the language and spirit of the law of every nation and undertake open and fair corporate activities to be a good corporate citizen of the world.
2. Respect the culture and customs of every nation and contribute to economic and social development through corporate activities in the communities.
3. Dedicate ourselves to providing clean and safe products and to enhancing the quality of life everywhere through all our activities.
4. Create and develop advanced technologies and provide outstanding products and services that fulfill the needs of customers worldwide.
5. Foster a corporate culture that enhances individual creativity and teamwork value while honoring mutual trust and respect between labor and management.
6. Pursue growth in harmony with the global community through innovative management.
7. Work with business partners in research and creation to achieve stable, long-term growth and mutual benefits, while keeping ourselves open to new partnerships.

(Toyota's guiding principles were updated in 1997 to reflect their evolution from the founding precepts established in 1934.)

APPENDIX B

||||||||||||||||||||||||||||||||||||||||||

The Toyota Way

Toyota established the Toyota Way guidelines in 2001 as a means of articulating the corporate mission to employees, which is based on two pillars: (1) continuous improvement, and (2) respect for people.

CONTINUOUS IMPROVEMENT

Challenge: We form a long-term vision, meeting challenges with courage and creativity to realize our dreams.

- Value through manufacturing and delivery of products and services
- Spirit of challenge
- Long-range perspective
- Thorough consideration in decision making

Kaizen: We improve our business operations continuously, always driving for innovation and evolution.

- *Kaizen* mind and innovative thinking
- Building lean systems and structure
- Promoting organizational learning

Genchi Genbutsu: We practice *genchi genbutsu:* go to the source to find the facts to make correct decisions, build consensus, and achieve goals at our best speed.

- *Genchi genbutsu*
- Effective consensus building
- Commitment to achievement

RESPECT FOR PEOPLE

Respect: We respect others, make every effort to understand each other, take responsibility, and do our best to build mutual trust.

- Respect for stakeholders
- Mutual trust and mutual responsibility
- Sincere communication

Teamwork: We stimulate personal and professional growth, share the opportunities of development, and maximize individual and team performance.

- Commitment to education and development
- Respect for the individual; realizing consolidated power as a team.

APPENDIX C

|||||||||||||||||||||||||||||||||||||||

Japanese Terms Used at Toyota

andon: Originates from the Japanese word for "lamp." Most commonly, andons are lights placed on machines or on production lines to indicate operation status. The andon cord is to be pulled to stop the process to ensure quality.

genjitsu: The facts or the reality; facts are the basis of sound decision making.

genchi genbutsu: "Go and see the problem firsthand." This is the belief that practical experience is valued over theoretical knowledge. You must see the problem to know the problem.

heijunka: In the production schedule, the overall leveling of the volume and of the variety of items produced at the final assembly line in given time periods. *Heijunka* is a prerequisite for "just-in-time delivery."

hoshin: Goals (with targets), and means for achieving the goals and targets, to address business priorities to move the organization to a new level of performance; variable from year to year; could also be multiyear; *hoshin* is developed by executive management.

horenso: A Toyota-invented acronym derived from the Japanese words *hokoku* (giving a thorough update to somebody), *renraku* (staying in touch on a subject), and *soudan* (consultation about an issue). *Horenso,* which when spoken sounds like the Japanese word for spinach, is a detailed progress report on issues or problems, and employees in Japan often say, "Did you remember your *horenso?*"

jidoka: One of the two main pillars of the Toyota Production System. *Jidoka* refers to the ability to stop production lines, by man or machine, in the event of problems such as equipment malfunction, quality issues, or late work. *Jidoka* helps prevent the passing of defects, helps identify and correct problem areas using localization and isolation, and makes it possible to build quality into the production process.

jishuken: Management-driven *kaizen*, or continuous improvement activity, where leadership identifies areas in need of continuous improvement and spreads the information through the organization to stimulate *kaizen* activity on specific initiatives.

kaizen: A system of continuous improvement in which instances of *muda* (waste) are eliminated one by one at minimal cost. This is performed by all employees rather than by specialists; every employee is responsible for contributing to continuous improvement.

mieruka: To make visible; bringing problems or facts into the open.

mondi kaiketsu: Problem solving; Toyota frequently holds multiday seminars for company employees focusing on effective *mondi kaiketsu.*

muda: Translated as "waste," or actions or processes where nonvalue is added. Primary types of *muda* include overproduction, waiting, conveyance, processing, inventory, motion, and correction. Fits with *muri* and *mura* as three things to avoid.

mura: Irregularity or nonstandardization; fits with *muda* and *muri* as three things to avoid.

muri: Overexertion; fits with *muda* and *mura* as three things to avoid.

namawashi: Preliminary work to involve other sections/departments in discussions to seek input, information, and/or support for a proposal or change (policy, etc.) that would affect them.

obeya: Big-room style of work; many employees working in an open space much like a United States newspaper newsroom. Advantages are that managers can easily see and hear what is going on daily;

disadvantages are that it can be harder for individuals to get work done in the distraction.

poka-yoke: Refers to a mistake-proofing device or procedure which prevents defects and protects quality during the production process.

soikufu: Creative workplace thinking, or capitalizing on workers' ideas.

takt time: The daily production number needed to meet orders in the system divided by the number of working hours in the day. *Takt* is the German word for the baton an orchestra conductor uses to keep beat. The term was adapted for use in manufacturing to determine production rate.

yokoten: Across everywhere; plant-related activities and/or countermeasures that are communicated plantwide and with other company affiliates; horizontally encompassing.

APPENDIX D

||||||||||||||||||||||||||||||||||||||||||||

Charting the Success

(Information provided by Dr. Chris Brockton, professor of finance at the University of Tennessee at Chattanooga, with the assistance of Dr. Judson W. Russell, CFA, finance professor at the University of North Carolina at Charlotte.)

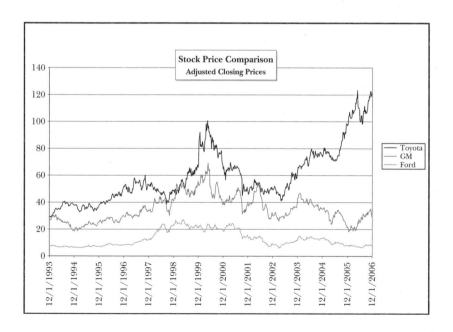

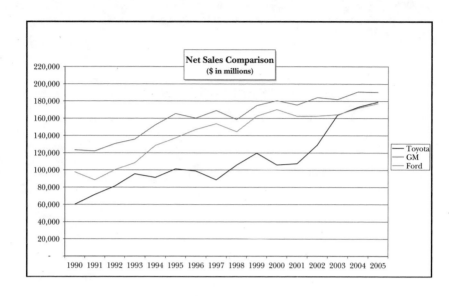

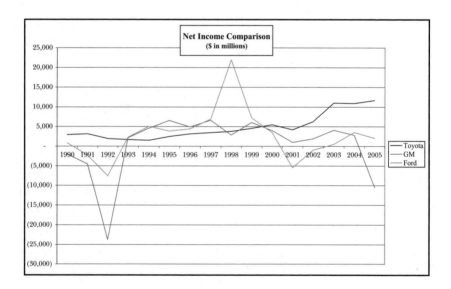

ACKNOWLEDGMENTS

The automotive industry is said to be one of the most cyclical in the world, but when I first began to investigate how Toyota became number one, I had a strong suspicion the story was bigger than simply one company overcoming its competitors. For Toyota to overtake General Motors as the largest automaker in the world is one thing; for Toyota to bring years of stability to an otherwise cyclical industry is another. So I reached out for help in qualifying exactly what Toyota has done from its humble beginning to today.

My call was to a university professor known for his passion and flair for numbers that tell the true story. We talked about what angles might be available for investigation and he went in search of data to compare and analyze. Dr. Chris Brockton, professor of finance at the University of Tennessee at Chattanooga, compiled this data with the assistance of Dr. Judson W. Russell, CFA, and finance professor at the University of North Carolina at Charlotte. Both Dr. Brockton and Dr. Russell are to be thanked and commended for their able assistance and for pointing out, in particular, with their data the fact that, contrary to popular belief, the automotive business, and manufacturing in general, does not have to be cyclical.

At Portfolio, working with editor Jeffrey Krames was a pleasure of the highest degree. I have admired his work for years and we had spoken occasionally, knowing the day would come when our paths would cross on just the right project. When this opportunity arose, we both knew immediately the timing was right to work together. Others at Portfolio who deserve mention are publisher Adrian Zackheim, widely known as one of the best in the book business; Will Weisser, who understands better than most how to get books into readers' hands; and Courtney Young, who helped me with many steps along the way from contract to completion, but, mostly, in completion. She and Jeffrey Krames did what many in publishing no longer do: edit. They worked extensively with the manuscript from top to bottom, reminding me that all works can and should be improved upon—some more than others. To Jeffrey and Courtney, I extend a most sincere thank you and appreciation for their partnership.

This manuscript would have not been complete without much help and cooperation from Toyota. I should note, though, before going too far, that the work was done in complete objectivity with no involvement or influence from the company other than cooperation in terms of interviews with key employees and executives when sought. To be granted such meaningful time with top executives in both the United States and Japan is much appreciated, and the openness contributed to my understanding of *How Toyota Became #1*. In the spirit of Toyota, I found that knowing and understanding is achieved through *genchi genbutsu* (going and seeing). Many thanks, then, to my hosts for a springtime visit to Japan, including Tomami Imai, Yurika Motoyoshi, and Paul Nolasco. I will long be grateful for their valuable assistance and openness. Also at Toyota, a sincere thank you to Mira Sleilati, who responded to too many e-mails, helped arrange vital interviews in the United States, and worked patiently with my continual curiosity.

A special thank you must also be given to my wife, Kent. Only a patient spouse can tolerate one who writes for a living and mine might be the most patient of all. For this manuscript, she endured not only the research and writing but also the pain of deadlines and efforts to get it right as time grew smaller and opportunity larger. What's more, she provided me with the larger inspiration to put words on paper in the first place. When she first suggested I turn passion into profession—writing books for a living—I bristled; now, upon completion of my eighth work, the idea does not seem so out of place. To her, I can only say every writer should be so fortunate.

Others who deserve mention from a long list of worthy candidates include: Albert Waterhouse, a friend and associate who finds as much thrill in inspiring business lessons as I; Henry Oehmig, a friend and faithful business associate; Craig Holley; Joe Ferguson; Mitchell Bell; Gordon Davenport; Ward Nelson; and Miller Welborn and Ward Petty, who loaned a perfect writing spot near the beach at just the right moment.

NOTES

||||||||||||||||||||||||||||||

Understanding a complex global business story like Toyota's requires an author to go directly to the source. The bulk of this book was crafted from my personal visits to Toyota facilities around the world and from interviews and discussions with Toyota employees and executives.

I visited Japan in March 2007 for Toyota plant and facility tours and key company interviews. I also made trips to New York (December 2006) for two interviews with Jim Press; Toyota's Georgetown, Kentucky, plant (December 2006) for an interview with Gary Convis; and Detroit, Michigan (January 2007), for interviews during the annual North American International Auto Show.

I also conducted dozens of other interviews with leading industry sources, including former Toyota employees, such as Dennis Cuneo, and employees of other global automakers. These discussions allowed me to develop the majority of this work from primary sources.

I've named sources directly quoted from firsthand interviews at the beginning of the notes for each appropriate chapter. Subsequent quotes from the same source in the same chapter are attributable to the initial citation. In addition to the Toyota executives I've specifically quoted, I was also able to talk with dozens of Toyota employees and managers during visits to facilities around the world. These many individuals, while not listed here, provided invaluable understanding, research, and background information.

In most instances, quotes appearing in the book are taken directly from the firsthand, one-on-one interviews. However, in a very few cases, clarifications of specific quotes occurred after interviews through e-mail exchange with the sources. In those cases, the primary interview date is still listed since that is when information was initially obtained. In instances where I quoted secondary sources to help tell the story of *How Toyota Became #1*, the source is duly noted.

Also, I'd like to emphasize that this book was written completely independent of Toyota. While Toyota was cooperative in making employees and executives available for interviews in both the United States and Japan, coordinating plant and facility tours, and responding to queries for research and background information, the company was not involved in the content or the manuscript in any way.

Chapter 1

7 **"If we only tried to achieve . . ."** Interview with Toyota executive vice president Mitsuo Kinoshita, Toyota City, Japan, March 2007.

11 **"The spirit of self-help . . ."** *Self-Help* (2002; Oxford University Press), by Samuel Smiles.

13 **". . . that youth must work . . ."** *Self-Help* (2002; Oxford University Press) by Samuel Smiles.

13 **"Everyone thinks of changing the world . . ."** See www.quotations page.com.

19 **"They have less ego . . ."** Interviews with Toyota Motor North America president Jim Press, New York, New York, December 2006.

Chapter 2

25 **"Something is wrong if . . ."** From *Reliable Plant*, March 2006.

28 **"I like being No. 1 . . ."** *New York Times*, January 5, 2007.

29 **"My mom and dad . . ."** Interview with senior executive adviser for Toyota Gary Convis, Georgetown, Kentucky, December 2006.

29 **"To me it was like . . ."** *Lexington Herald Leader*, November 20, 2006.

30 **"You don't cut corners . . ."** Interview with senior executive adviser for Toyota Gary Convis, Georgetown, Kentucky, December 2006.

31 **"The factory is the most visible . . ."** Interview with Toyota Motor North America president Jim Press, New York, New York, December 2006.

38 **"But one thing was . . ."** Telephone interview with former NUMMI employee Steve Bera, November 2006.

40 **"What we do . . ."** Interview with senior executive adviser for Toyota Gary Convis, Georgetown, Kentucky, December 2006.

41 **"People try to adapt . . ."** Telephone interview with former Toyota executive and Toyota consultant Dennis Cuneo, February 2006.

43 **"There is not a day . . ."** See www.deming.org, text from 1991 Deming Prize ceremony.

Chapter 3

47 **"Once you buy into . . ."** Interview with Toyota executive vice president Gary Convis, Georgetown, Kentucky, December 2006.

49 **"It's my favorite time . . ."** *Battle Creek Inquirer,* February 22, 2006.

52 **"Why?"** Interview with Toyota Motor North America president Jim Press, New York, New York, December 2006.

58 **"When we start . . ."** Interview with Koki Konishi, director of the Toyota Institute, Toyota City, Japan, March 2007.

Chapter 4

59 **"A place for everything . . ."** See www.brainyquote.com.

63 **"Toyota is proud of its . . ."** Interview with Toyota Motor North America president Jim Press, New York, New York, December 2006.

68 **"We believe that human beings . . ."** Interview with Toyota executive vice president Mitsuo Kinoshita, Toyota City, Japan, March 2007.

69 **"People thought it was strange . . ."** *Time,* July 2005.

69 **"Look, there are . . ."** Ibid.

Chapter 5

73 **"The world-class quality . . ."** *Toronto Star,* February 18, 2007.

75 **"If there is a problem . . ."** Interviews with Toyota Motor North America president Jim Press, New York, New York, December 2006.

78 **"Why don't all the . . ."** *Wall Street Journal,* December 22, 2006.

78 **"We don't share everything . . ."** Ibid.

79 **"It is always interesting . . ."** Interview with senior executive adviser for Toyota Gary Convis, Georgetown, Kentucky, December 2006.

Chapter 6

85 **"[Toyota] somehow said . . ."** *Car* (1997; W. W. Norton and Company), by Mary Walton.

86 **"we don't have to tell people . . ."** Interview with Toyota Motor North America president Jim Press, New York, New York, December 2006.

86 **"Can we create a . . ."** *Lexus: The Relentless Pursuit* (2004: John Wiley & Sons), by Chester Dawson.

87 **"This car is not something . . ."** *The Toyota Way* (2003; McGraw-Hill), by Jeffrey Liker.

88 **". . . 60 designers, 24 engineering . . ."** *Lexus: The Relentless Pursuit* (2004: John Wiley & Sons), by Chester Dawson.

97 **"Deliver a product . . ."** *Car* (1997; W. W. Norton and Company), by Mary Walton.

97 **"Did Toyoda . . ."** Ibid.

Chapter 7

103 **"Great results cannot be achieved . . ."** *Self-Help* (2002; Oxford University Press), by Samuel Smiles.

104 **"We would not . . ."** Interview with Toyota Motor North America president Jim Press, New York, New York, December 2006.

105 **"Our foundation is . . ."** Interview with senior executive adviser for Toyota Gary Convis, Georgetown, Kentucky, December 2006.

109 **"There will be great . . ."** *Fortune,* February 21, 2006.

110 **"[Toyota's Japanese leadership] . . ."** Interview with Toyota Motor Sales USA senior vice president Don Esmond, Detroit, Michigan, January 2007.

111 **"Hybrids today are not . . ."** Associated Press, December 7, 2006, www.associatedpress.com.

113 **"It's really one of those . . ."** Associated Press, May 12, 2006, www.associatedpress.com.

113 **"Based on all . . ."** Interview with Toyota Motor North America president Jim Press, New York, New York, December 2006.

Chapter 8

117 **"We make things . . ."** *Time*, July 25, 2005.

117 **"We know we . . ."** Interviews with Toyota Motor North America president Jim Press, New York, New York, December 2006.

118 **GM executives claimed . . .** *Comeback* (1994; Simon & Schuster), by Joseph White and Paul Ingrassia.

119 **"I'm not concerned about . . ."** *Car* (1997; W. W. Norton and Company), by Mary Walton.

120 **"We're a company that listens . . ."** *New York Times*, January 4, 2007.

123 **"We want to capture . . ."** Reuters, February 7, 2007, www .reuters.com

123 **"From my perspective . . ."** Interview with Toyota Motor Sales USA senior vice president Don Esmond, Detroit, Michigan, January 2007.

125 **"Whenever you do a global . . ."** *New York Times*, February 10, 2007.

127 **"All the old rules are gone . . ."** *New York Times*, September 16, 2006.

Chapter 9

131 **"When the decision . . ."** Interviews with Toyota Motor North America president Jim Press, New York, New York, December 2006.

136 **"We had to move . . ."** Telephone interview with former NUMMI employee Steve Bera, November 2006.

137 **"I remember when . . ."** Interview with senior executive adviser for Toyota Gary Convis, Georgetown, Kentucky, December 2006.

138 **"If NUMMI did . . ."** Telephone interview with former Toyota executive and Toyota consultant Dennis Cuneo, February 2006.

140 **Supply shipments were in disarray . . .** *Ward's Auto World*, January 1996.

Chapter 10

143 **"It is a mistake to suppose . . ."** *Self-Help* (2002; Oxford University Press), by Samuel Smiles.

144 **"You don't blame employees . . ."** *Battle Creek Inquirer*, February 22, 2006.

146 **"You don't learn from . . ."** Interviews with Toyota Motor North America president Jim Press, New York, New York, December 2006.

148 **"There was always . . ."** *Fast Company*, December/January 2007.

149 **"I started out . . ."** Ibid.

150 **"I have come to understand . . ."** Ibid.

151 **"Toyota's quality has . . ."** Bloomberg, June 23, 2006, www .bloomberg.com.

151 **"Problems must be made . . ."** *Business Week*, March 5, 2007.

151 **"Early detection . . ."** Ibid.

152 **"I believe it is vital . . ."** *New York Times*, December 23, 2006.

Chapter 11

154 **The result was . . .** *City Journal*, summer 1995.

157 **"That is a good . . ."** Telephone interview with former Toyota executive and Toyota consultant Dennis Cuneo, February 2006.

158 **"I remember going . . ."** Telephone interview with former NUMMI employee Steve Bera, November 2006.

159 **"GM and Ford . . ."** Interview with Tennessee congressman Zach Wamp, Chattanooga, Tennessee, November 2006.

Chapter 12

161 **"The true measurement . . ."** Interviews with Toyota Motor North America president Jim Press, New York, New York, December 2006.

167 **"The duty of helping one's self . . ."** *Self-Help* (2002; Oxford University Press), by Samuel Smiles.

168 **"Toyota is now . . ."** Telephone interview with former Toyota executive and Toyota consultant Dennis Cuneo, February 2006.

170 **"To sustain growth . . ."** Interview with Toyota executive vice president Mitsuo Kinoshita, Toyota City, Japan, March 2007.

171 **"At Toyota, a doing person . . ."** Interview with director of the Toyota Institute Koki Konishi, Toyota City, Japan, March 2007.

Chapter 13

173 **"If employees just did . . ."** Interview with Toyota executive vice president Mitsuo Kinoshita, Toyota City, Japan, March 2007.
175 **Calling Toyota "the finest . . ."** Associated Press, January 4, 2007, www.associatedpress.com.
177 **"I thought about that . . ."** *Battle Creek Inquirer*, February 22, 2006.
178 **"On our board . . ."** Interview with senior executive adviser for Toyota Gary Convis, Georgetown, Kentucky, December 2006.
183 **"each of its four . . ."** *New York Times*, February 8, 2007.

Chapter 14

185 **"We begin to create . . ."** Interview with senior executive adviser for Toyota Gary Convis, Georgetown, Kentucky, December 2006.
186 **"The apprenticeship . . ."** *Self-Help* (2002; Oxford University Press), by Samuel Smiles.
187 **"Toyota executives . . ."** Interview with director of the Toyota Institute Koki Konishi, Toyota City, Japan, March 2007.
188 **"We want to have . . ."** Interview with Toyota executive vice president Mitsuo Kinoshita, Toyota City, Japan, March 2007.
190 **"People either have it . . ."** Interviews with Toyota Motor North America president Jim Press, New York, New York, December 2006.
191 **"We do not accept . . ."** Interview with senior executive adviser for Toyota Gary Convis, Georgetown, Kentucky, December 2006.
191 **"For Americans or anyone . . ."** *New York Times*, February 15, 2007.
193 **"It is one of . . ."** Interview with Toyota executive vice president Mitsuo Kinoshita, Toyota City, Japan, March 2007.

Chapter 15

195 **"I feel that being successful may . . ."** *Business Week*, February 10, 2005.

196 **"We always plan . . ."** Interviews with Toyota Motor North America president Jim Press, New York, New York, December 2006.

196 **"There are grounds . . ."** *New York Times*, December 23, 2006.

197 **"They worry about details . . ."** *Detroit Free Press*, February 8, 2007.

197 **"Everyone should be dissatisfied . . ."** *Time*, July 25, 2005.

Conclusion

205 **"Our goal is . . ."** Interviews with Toyota Motor North America president Jim Press, New York, New York, December 2006.

207 **"Sales volume and market . . ."** *Guardian*, March 31, 2006.

INDEX

||||||||||||||||||||||||||||